To Call It Home

To Call It Home

The New Immigrants of Southwestern Minnesota

by

Joseph A. Amato

with

John Meyer, John Radzilowski,
Donata DeBruyckere, and Anthony Amato

To Call It Home was a report originally written for the Southwest Leadership for Local Elected and Appointed Persons Project (LEAP). It was revised and prepared for publication by Crossings Press.

The first 500 copies of this book were funded by the sponsors of the conference, "To Call It Home," held October 18, 1996, at Southwest State University, Marshall, Minnesota.

Second printing, 1997

Published by:

Crossings Press
P.O. Box 764
Marshall, MN 56258

ISBN 0-9614119-7-X

Cover photo is courtesy of the *Independent* of Marshall.
The Heartland employee pictured is Apolinar Rocha.

To all migrants who have
made long journeys in body and mind,
especially Rosalia and Frances.

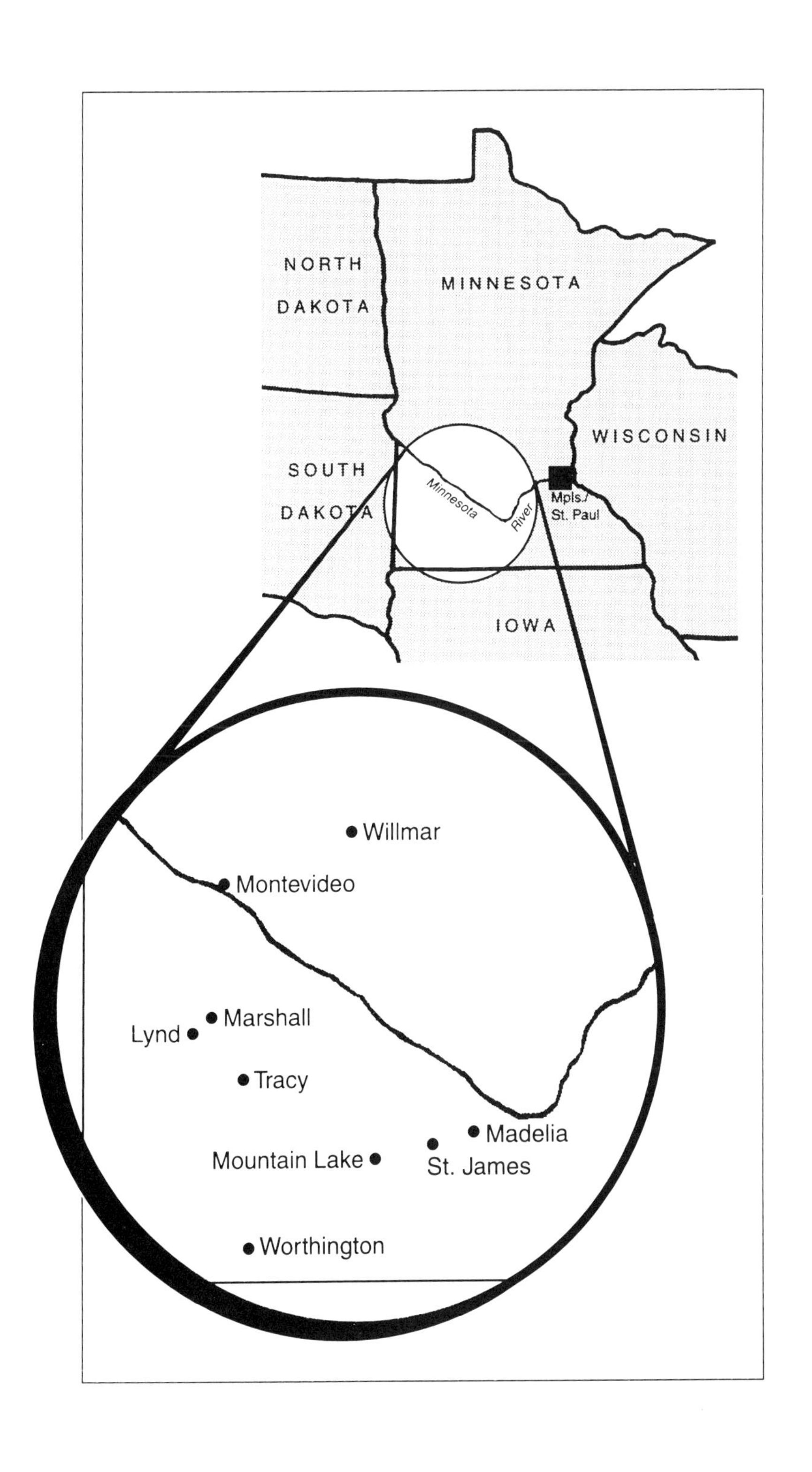
NORTH
DAKOTA
MINNESOTA
WISCONSIN
SOUTH
DAKOTA
Minnesota
River
Mpls./
St. Paul
IOWA
Willmar
Montevideo
Marshall
Lynd
Tracy
Madelia
Mountain Lake
St. James
Worthington

Contents

Index of Tables

Index of Graphs

Preface and Acknowledgments

I am indebted to Southwest Leadership for Local Elected and Appointed Persons Project (LEAP) for asking me to write this study of immigrant newcomers. It involves a transformation of this region on a scale exceeding all other changes except for its original European settlements. While the newcomers themselves must ask such fundamental questions as what is this new place to which they have come and whether or not they can, and will, eventually call it home, the leaders of the host community must confront equally portentous issues. They must ask who the newcomers are, and they must ask of their source, which is the new and emerging regional beef and poultry industries. These industries, first seen as an answer to the farm crisis and overall rural decline of the 1980s, are now understood to test regional leaders' institutions, policies, and very abilities to foster worthwhile change.

For the chance to write of this great transformation, I owe special thanks to several of LEAP's prime movers: Worthington Mayor Robert Demuth, who wishes his town and newcomers well; Marshall Mayor Robert Byrnes, who is as energetic and faithful a guardian as any city could wish; City Administrator Joseph McCabe of Madelia and Director of Community Services Harry Weilage of Marshall, whose energy and goodwill are admirable assets to their respective communities; and Minnesota Extension Service, University of Minnesota, leadership specialists Mary Ann Gwost Hennen of St. Paul and Sara Taylor of Nobles County, whose long-term dedication to the project kept it afloat. Also special thanks are extended to executive officers of Southwest State University: Vice President for Advancement James Babcock, who encouraged me to seize this opportunity and continued to support me at every stage of its conception and formulation; and President Douglas Sweetland and Academic Vice President Randy Abbott, who saw the importance of Regional Studies in Southwest State's mission to the region.

Many of the above, and others as well, earned my gratitude for having allayed my anxiety, which was made keen by the six-month deadline for researching and writing this report. On bad days they made me feel like the alligator that Brer Rabbit promised to show something interesting. "Brer Rabbit (I speak as if I am the alligator) had done lured me out into the center of small grassy meadow with der promise to show me der something interesting, and den he done set it on all sides on fire." Amidst smoke and flame, I felt lucky to escape with only the white of my stomach singed. On good days, which outnumbered bad days, I felt like Brer Rabbit himself. I cheered myself for having fooled them into throwing me into the terrible thorn patch (of research and writing) where I thrive. They were paying me to do just what I wanted to do.

For twenty years I have harnessed together, under the yoke of my job as a college teacher, my training as a European cultural historian and my belief that this region is worthy of study. I won't say anything here about my training, but I will say a little about my belief in regional and rural studies, which blesses me with the unique opportunity of doing the good and the pleasing at the same time.

The first premise of regional studies was established twenty years ago with former SSU History Department colleagues. It asserted that the rural world is not an inferior object of study. The historian should study it with the same care with which he or she would undertake any other subject. The reward for doing this will be the discovery that regional history is a rich form of history, even if its audiences are smaller and less tolerant of academic theory. This first premise was underpinned by a second premise: The study of the past is practical. It increases understanding and awareness of human life which, in turn, strengthen common sense in people of intelligence and good character.

For all its limits, the study of history remains the best way to grasp the present. It allows one to distinguish between what is old and what is new, what is fundamental and what is transient, what has changed, how it has changed, and upon which conditions it abides. Such an understanding proves crucial for practical judgment and action, which are the fundamental activities for leaders.

To Call It Home should serve the practical purposes of regional leaders. It offers them knowledge of the immigrant newcomers, among whom are included a variety of Africans, Asians, and Hispanics. It responds to such questions as who the newcomers are, why they came, and, to a lesser degree, what they experience upon arrival here. It gives special attention to the matters of social services, housing, school, and crime, which concerned the corresponding LEAP committees. It describes the newcomers' patterns of migrations and their tie to the region's emerging meat and poultry industries. At the same time, it examines the contemporary discourse, attitudes, and arguments surrounding immigrant newcomers.

Of unique value, the study compares the diverse experiences of several different food-processing cities in southwestern Minnesota. Included in this study are the region's three largest cities, Willmar, Worthington, and Marshall; two of Marshall's neighboring cities, Tracy and Lynd, where many Marshall newcomers reside; and Madelia, Mountain Lake, St. James, and Montevideo, which are uniquely dependent on the newcomers. It culminates after mention of Montevideo, which has just opened a turkey plant, and with Willmar, the region's largest city, which houses the largest food-processing industry.

On the basis of a comparison of these cities, *To Call It Home* suggests that there is, at least in outline, a general pattern to this new experience, which begins to emerge even after five or six years. However, it also suggests that at the same time, each city has had, for a variety of reasons, different experiences and should, accordingly, follow different future policies and strategies. Furthermore, this comparison should help civic leaders assess the immediate and long-term place of immigrant newcomers in their individual community; appraise the particular connection between new industries and the newcomers in their town; establish a community-wide dialogue based on fundamental facts and shared perspectives; and, finally, develop policies and plans for the good of newcomers and lifelong residents alike.

The search for a comparative understanding not only defines the study but underlines the planning of the forthcoming region-wide conference that will be held at Southwest State University in October 1996. The conference will be financially supported by the university, its Gunlogson Regional Research Fund, its Regional Studies Program, and Minnesota Extension Service, University of Minnesota. It will also be supported by the cities of Marshall and Worthington, the Otto Bremer Foundation, the Minnesota Humanities Commission, and our own Society for the Study of Local and Regional History, which in the past five years has sponsored a variety of annual conferences on regional life. At the conference, our book, *To Call It Home,* will be presented to the public for the first time. There will be national experts on recent migration patterns in the Midwest, particularly Mexicans and Mexican Americans, the growth of the meat and poultry industries in the rural Midwest, and the experiences of comparable food-processing communities in Nebraska and Iowa. The conference will also feature southwest Minnesota civic leaders describing and comparing their individual town's recent experiences, present problems, and future hopes for making their communities a home for all peoples.

In writing the book and planning the conference, I have been profoundly dependent on the collaboration of colleagues and friends who deserve deep thanks. John Meyer, who coauthored with me *The Decline of Rural Minnesota,* provided this work with its demographics and charts. John Radzilowski, who has worked with me on *The Great Jerusalem Artichoke Circus* and *A New College on the Prairie,* wrote significant sections of the study, in addition to providing the bibliography. Krystal Johnson critically read the section on the Somalis. Anthony Amato, my son, interrupted the writing of his dissertation on Carpathian mountaineers to write the section on Montevideo and Willmar. Donata DeBruyckere, as fine an assistant as anyone ever had, helped research and write important sections of this book. Along with Donata and Anthony, Jan Louwagie, head of the university's History Center and the moving spirit behind the Society for the Study of Local and Regional History, again cheerfully found herself helping us plan another large conference.

Professor Don Stull, anthropologist at the University of Kansas, and author of a recent volume on the meat-processing industry—*Any Way You Cut It*—deserves special acknowledgment for his excellent job of "slicing up" our report and providing the conference with its particular focus on meat packing in Lexington, Nebraska. John Kostishack, Executive Director of the Otto Bremer Foundation, served us doubly. He not only supplied the grant that paid for several of the conference's speakers but he critically read the manuscript. Jim Tate, editor of the Marshall *Independent*, provided the photograph used on the cover. Marianne Zarzana, SSU University Relations, edited the manuscript, and Scott Perrizo, of Crossings Press Publishing Services, helped design the book. As in the case of many publications, Kathy Wenzel of the Jackson *Livewire* played an important role in the design and the production of the book. Rhonda Fedde, of SSU's Duplicating Center, again unstintingly labored on our behalf.

While we cannot mention by name all who helped us, we would like to express our appreciation to everyone who supplied us with information and materials. We especially thank those who participated in the large group interviews in Marshall, St. James, Worthington, and Madelia. Likewise, thanks go to those in Tracy, Mountain Lake, Worthington, Lynd, and St. James who participated in lengthy telephone interviews.

Without any intention of forgetting individual and group participants, we would particularly like to mention the following leaders: mayors Brian Peltier of Lynd, John Almlie of Tracy, Robert Byrnes of Marshall, Robert Demuth of Worthington, Terry Stone of Madelia, and Robert Kline of St. James; school administrators Kent Nelson of St. James, Gerald Huber of Marshall, and Gary Brandt of Worthington; and law enforcement officers Marvin Bahn of Marshall, Donovan Mickelson of St. James, Donald Linssen of Worthington, and Jim Kulset and Julie Asmus of Willmar. Gratitude is also owed to early LEAP leaders Jan Rhode, Minnesota School Boards Association; Mary Sabatke, Government Training Service; Sharon Roe Anderson, Reflective Leadership Center of the Humphrey Institute; Merry Beckmann, Association of Minnesota Counties; and Sharon Klumpp, League of Minnesota Cities.

Information from Campbell Soup Company and Swift & Company, both of Worthington, was particularly helpful. Jim Tate of the Marshall *Independent* and Forrest Peterson, Donna Middleton, and David Little of the Willmar *West Central Tribune* were truly generous in providing news articles. Many city, county, state, and private agencies provided valuable information.

As in most things, my wife and friends bore the hidden costs of being on familiar terms with Brer Rabbit and "Brer Alligator."

Introduction

Home for some is a place. For others, it is a memory. For others still it is a hope. Like the Jews of the Old Testament, many know themselves by their journey toward home. All of us are migrants or the children of migrants. Only people with short memories forget their migrations.

The United States is an immigrant nation. Most Americans are descendants of immigrants. From earliest times, the lands that became the United States were settled by peoples of many backgrounds. The first to come were the ancestors of today's American Indians, who discovered the New World in the dim past of the Pleistocene. In the seventeenth and eighteenth centuries, English, Scots, Germans, French, Irish, Dutch, and Welsh settled much of what is now the eastern United States. In the eighteenth century, millions of slaves were brought from Africa and the Caribbean islands to labor on the plantations of the South. A second major wave of immigrants came from Europe throughout the nineteenth century and included the peoples of the British Isles, Germany, and Scandinavia. They were joined by Chinese, Japanese, French and British Canadians, and Mexicans, many of whom became American citizens when the United States annexed the Southwest and California in the middle of the nineteenth century. By the end of the nineteenth century and the beginning of the twentieth, a vast new wave of people arrived from eastern and southern Europe: Italians, Poles, Jews, Greeks, Slovaks, Czechs, South Slavs, East Slavs, Arabs, and others.

With the arrival of these new peoples—many of whom were very different from previous waves—came a reaction against the newcomers from those already on these shores. This was often manifested in anti-Catholicism and, later, anti-Semitism. The Irish first bore the brunt of this anti-immigrant reaction. Later, new racial theories, which held that northern and western European Protestants were superior to other peoples, were used to justify discrimination against blacks, Asians, Italians, Poles, Jews, Mexicans, and others. Germans, too, felt the sting of prejudice during World War I. These sentiments led to laws that stopped immigration from countries whose populations were considered racially inferior. Immigrants already in this country were severely pressured to give up their cultures, religions, and languages. Still, these newcomers, who often modeled themselves on dominant host cultures, through generations of hard work and sacrifice, achieved success in the United States. In spite of the tremendous pressures to assimilate, their descendants remember their ethnic origins. In the 1990 census, less than 6 percent listed "white" or "American" when asked their ethnic origin or ancestry.[1]

The recent history of the United States has continued this immigrant story. Since World War II, immigration to the U.S. has steadily increased. Although recent decades have seen a surge in immigration from eastern Europe, the Middle East, and Africa, since the 1970s this newest immigration has drawn its greatest numbers from Latin America and Asia. Latinos have come primarily from Mexico, Guatemala, El Salvador, and Cuba. They have been joined by citizen-migrants from Puerto Rico. Most Asian newcomers have arrived from the Philippines, Vietnam, Laos, Cambodia, Korea, and China.

The impact of this newest wave of immigrants has been considerably smaller than that of the previous immigrant wave in the period between 1870–1920. Then, immigrants were arriving at a rate of 10 for every 1,000 residents; in the 1980s, they came at a rate of 3.5 for every thousand. Only 8 percent of the U.S. population was foreign born in 1990, com-

---

[1]Rudolph J. Vecoli, ed. *Gale Encyclopedia of Multicultural America* (New York: Gale Research Inc., 1995), 1:xxii–xxiii.

pared to 15 percent in 1910.[2] Despite this, immigration has once again become a topic of heated debate. Of particular concern has been the arrival of illegal immigrants. These undocumented arrivals make up only about 15 percent of all immigrants, and most are concentrated in just a few states. Currently, immigrants contribute about $70.3 billion in taxes to federal and state government while receiving $42.9 billion in services such as education and welfare.[3]

The new arrivals, who like earlier immigrant groups tend to have high birth rates, are helping to further transform the American population. Presently, American Indians constitute less than 1 percent of the U.S. population, Asians 3 percent, Hispanics 10 percent, and African Americans 12 percent. On the basis of present trends, the Census Bureau forecasts that by 2050 Hispanics will increase to 22 percent of the population, while Asians will be 10 percent, and African Americans 14 percent.

The history of Minnesota mirrors the national story of migration. Its first residents were American Indians, who themselves had made, and continued to make, long and complex migrations in a land of less fixed borders. The arrival of European Americans brought dozens of new groups to the state. The Minnesota state constitution was originally printed in English and several other languages, including Welsh. By 1896, official election instructions were being issued in nine languages: English, German, Norwegian, Swedish, Finnish, French, Czech, Italian, and Polish. In 1910 over half the people living in most counties of southwestern Minnesota had been born outside the United States.[4]

Minnesota remains a destination for immigrants and migrants. In the 1980s, the state's small Asian population increased dramatically. The percentage of government-defined minorities, including African Americans and American Indi-

[2]Ibid., 1:xxiv.

[3]Jeffrey Passel and Rebecca Clark, "How Much Do Immigrants Really Cost? A Reappraisal of Huddle's 'The Cost of Immigrants,'" Urban Institute, Washington, D.C., Feb. 1994, p. 1.

[4]*Lyon County Reporter*, Oct. 17, 1896, supplement.

ans, grew to 5.6 percent of the state's total population in 1990, up from 3.4 percent in 1980. The largest increase of these groups was in the Twin Cities. Of the 300,000 people the state added, 22,000 were Hispanics, while 100,000 were either black, Asian, or American Indian. (These figures were disputed by some minority advocates. Hispanic organizations, for example, estimated their population at 69,000.)[5]

The growth of government-defined minorities has been slower in southwestern Minnesota than in the Twin Cities metropolitan area. In 1990, Latinos made up 4.92 percent of the population of Lyon, Jackson, Nobles, Cottonwood, and Watonwan counties; Asians made up 2.22 percent, and blacks made up about 1 percent. Since the 1990 census, the number of newcomers has dramatically increased.

Like previous immigrants, recent newcomers to Minnesota come from different continents and social classes. They have different cultures and educational levels. From war-ravaged southeast Asia come the families of educated Vietnamese officers, Laotian officers and soldiers, and Hmong farmers and hunters who fought against the North Vietnamese. From faction-torn east Africa come Somalis and Ethiopians. From both sides of the Rio Grande come Latinos.

Although equally attracted by the promise of work, these newcomers are strangers to one another, ignorant of the place and people to which they have arrived, and fearful that their own children will become strangers to them. They have come at different points in their journeys, with different governmental and church aid (if any), with varying reasons for coming and with different expectations for eventually returning home or establishing a new home. Some come as short-term workers, others know where they want to finally end up, while others only know they have no hope of ever returning home. Few yet know how southwestern Minnesota fits into their family's story of migration and home.

Newcomers enter southwestern Minnesota on different trajectories. They are so different and often move through so

[5]Paul Klauda and Suzanne P. Kelly, "Minority Population is Changing [the] Face of [the] State," *Star Tribune*, Minneapolis, Feb. 22, 1991, p. 1A.

rapidly that they are not easily observed even by those who care to look. They are, from one point of view, fellow humans deserving sympathetic understanding. They deserve all the help they can get from private groups and established institutions. They are, from a less generous point of view, needed labor for growing industry or mere warm bodies to shore up an aging and declining rural region. Coarse federal government categories, which both unify and distinguish people by race, geography, and historically nonexistent cultural categories, feed misperception and stereotypes in the host communities, which are predisposed to look at the newcomers through nativist, anti-Catholic, and racist lenses. National debates over welfare, crime, affirmative action, the primacy of English, and immigration have encouraged the tendency to view the newcomers in terms of abstract ideas and arguments.

Members of host communities—who forget that they themselves are the grandchildren of recent arrivals and members of diverse cultures—have no clear idea of who the newcomers are, how many are in the region, and whether they will stay. They have no model, even if their own families were once immigrants with similar experiences, to understand how these newcomers may live generations in a place, while heart and home are elsewhere for them. Members of the host communities have not been taught to understand how many people live provisionally in one place, until new possibilities or stern necessities lead them elsewhere. They lack an understanding of how the newcomers will choose to call a place home.

A higher standard of knowledge and action falls on the leaders of host communities. The leaders must have greater knowledge of who the newcomers are, and what their experiences and desires are. Leaders must not only welcome the newcomers but continue to strive to understand, help, and explain them to their new neighbors. They must also explain the receiving community to the newcomers. The leaders of towns that want to grow must try to transform some portion of the newcomers into residents and citizens.

Initially, individual leaders saw the new minorities differently. Some saw in them the promise of renewal. New people meant new growth, more business, and revitalized schools and institutions. Leaders in Madelia, Tracy, Mountain Lake, and elsewhere in the region saw the newcomers as essential to their long-term survival. In Worthington, leaders awoke in the early 1990s to a dramatic and continuing change whose direction and outcome they find disturbingly uncertain. In Marshall, leaders welcomed an industry, but left the newcomers to find housing elsewhere, which they did in nearby Tracy and Lynd.

Leaders did not come together to formulate concerted policies about the newcomers in a given town or region. In truth, leaders are not a clearly defined group in cities or the region as a whole. Furthermore, there is no vehicle for sharing of experiences and policies. In their cities, leaders held no forums about the newcomers, who they were, and what should be done for and about them. For better or worse, they did not hold the type of meetings that recently occurred in Spencer, Iowa, and nearby Iowa towns regarding the opening of a new meat-processing plant. In Spencer, the entire community (mixing real economic and civic concerns with rancor, nativism, and racism) debated and rejected the proposed plant around the issue of zoning. Instead, regional leaders here have welcomed new and expanding industries without reservations, letting the newcomers arrive as they would and residents react as they would.

Despite this laissez-faire approach, leaders still had to deal with many issues. Fundamental and inescapable questions surround housing, law enforcement, social welfare, and education. Language proved a large and expensive issue for courts, schools, and social services. (Of special concern was the question of why taxpayers should finance education in a second language.) There was a host of complaints centering around cultural misunderstandings. For instance, they focused on driving styles of Somalis in Marshall; Mexicans repairing their cars on their front lawns in St. James; Hmong hunting and courting styles in the vicinity of Marshall; and Asian fishing styles in Worthington. Of course, the actions and policies of the newcomers' primary employers—which have involved strikes and at least nine Immigration and Naturalization Service (INS) raids in the region since 1992—also embroiled leaders in the issues of their new minorities. Minneapolis and St. Paul newspapers added a sting to leaders' consciences when lengthy feature articles held local leaders accountable for what was happening to newcomers in their cities.

By a mixture of circumstances, goodwill, civic pride, and economic self-interest, local leaders had to acknowledge that they needed to find out who the newcomers were, what they meant for the future of local communities, and what should be done on their behalf. To put their own situation in context, they recognized the need to understand their situation in comparison to that of other cities in the region.

This mounting need led to the creation of a collaborative project called Leadership for Local Elected and Appointed Persons Project (LEAP). Primarily funded by Minnesota Extension Service and supported by Southwest State University's Regional Studies Program, a range of civic, social, and educational leaders from five counties—Nobles, Cottonwood, Jackson, Watonwan, and Lyon—formed LEAP in 1994. In consultation with representatives of newcomer communities, LEAP staked out four committee areas—leadership development, housing, law enforcement, and access and advocacy. In fall 1995, they commissioned this report.

Methodology

This report is meant to serve as a guide for elected and appointed officials and other leaders in southwestern Minnesota. This study focused on Marshall, Worthington, and Madelia, whose leadership was most active in LEAP. We also examined Tracy, Mountain Lake, and St. James as cities in LEAP's five-county area that have large and distinct groups of newcomers. We also made reference to Willmar, whose Latino community is the largest in southwestern Minnesota. We intended to furnish leaders of these towns with basic descriptions of the newcomers and to describe their cities' responses to them. We also sought to furnish officials and leaders with basic numbers, essential definitions, practical language, and primary distinctions for shaping and explaining common city, county, and regional policies regarding the newcomers.

To accomplish this we explored a number of complex things. The very assignment of offering a profile of the new minorities is difficult because most appeared after the 1990 census, which failed to count many new, undocumented, and migrant members. A study of newcomers to this region not only forced us to study very recent migrants but also workers belonging to an industry with one of the highest labor force turnover rates in the nation. We supplemented and extended census records with industrial and school records. Additionally, we calculated population turnover and migration patterns of the new immigrants, while utilizing formulas for living wages and suggesting a measure of the proportion and rate at which migrants are settling in a community.

This study involved a range of interviews with leaders of

all sorts, attendance at a variety of meetings, extensive correspondence with experts, and a great deal of other research. But it was not based on field studies of individual communities or their new residents. Consequently, it does not capture the richness of host communities, the diversity of both the permanent residents and the minority newcomers, and their everyday interactions. Likewise, we leaned toward analysis and did not explore or capture all the poignant tales of individual and group sacrifice; acts of generosity and kindness; painful stories of strikes, misunderstanding, and prejudice; and tragedies like fires in trailer courts and cruel murders. Nor, finally, does this study draw comparisons between southwestern Minnesota and the rest of the state and the Midwest.[1]

These limits did not stifle our presumption to direct leaders to what we defined as the core issue of leadership: the cost and means of turning a significant percentage of newcomers into community residents. This issue comes with two other fundamental questions: What is the likelihood newcomers can be transformed into permanent residents—or more precisely, encouraged to call this place home? Which social policies and actions (if any) should be aimed at the newcomers and which should be aimed at the laboring class as a whole?

Other questions come to mind. Can community leaders form a creative consensus on the matter of minorities? Even with intelligence and unified will, can they influence such significant factors as work, housing, and attitudes of the host community, which shape newcomers' decisions both to come and stay in a community? Finally, can they influence local businesses in general, and the large employers of newcomers in particular, to help the community turn newcomers into long-term residents?

---

[1]This study could be read in conjunction with two 1995 studies. The Stanford Study explores the rate of assimilation of minorities in southern California, while the Wilder Foundation report, based on over 600 interviews of Hispanics in Minnesota, raises a set of interesting questions and provides information that will prove useful in any future research on Mexicans and Mexican Americans in rural Minnesota.

Some evidence from certain sites in our region promises that a percentage of new immigrants will take root. They will stay; they will purchase trailers and homes; their children will do well in school; they will join the work force and the community as fully as any other group. This evidence, however, is insufficient to predict what will happen in any one community; nor does it indicate clearly what policies any given community should follow. This promising pattern can be aimed at and hoped for. Surely it must be measured and judged.

No one—and no single community—owns the future. But each community must act as if it can know and define itself. To do this, communities, caught up in a transformation of a size and scale exceeded only by the era of their historical founding and formation, need in-depth profiles of themselves. More simply, they need good, critical histories of their past. Around these stories they can rally their energies and hopes. Without these stories they cannot awaken the needed energy, imagination, and will of a new generation of leaders. Each community needs to compare its story and its own experiences with those of other regional and Midwestern communities. Every community needs to look in the mirror of other places to see and take measure of itself.

Each community that hopes to succeed must realize that benefits from growth and increased diversity are not without a cost. In varying degrees, communities will encounter complex sets of problems associated with housing shortages, high turnover rates, demands for increased health and social services, and a need of an expanded infrastructure. At the same time, communities at some point will be forced to adopt policies and adapt strategies to deal with the large new companies which hire newcomers and profoundly shape the future of the city.

Additionally, to borrow from a recent report on Lexington, Nebraska—a town profoundly changed in the last five years by an Iowa beef-processing plant—each community must help establish a "positive context of reception," which depends, in addition to a favorable immigration policy, on positive attitudes on the part of the host community, including established residents who share the background of the newcomers and the support of employers.[2]

Finally, each community needs to begin to act in light of its own vision of a larger, better, and more prosperous future. Such actions and visions fulfill leaders' obligations to newcomers and existing residents alike. Acceptance, intelligence, courage, and democracy are primary obligations for all who wish to be neighbors.

---

[2]The phrase "positive context of reception" derives from Alejandro Portes and József Böröcz, "Contemporary Immigration: Theoretical Perspectives on its Determinants and Modes of Incorporation," International Migration Review, 23 (3) (1989), 606–30. Its elaboration and application were found in Lourdes Gouveia and Donald Stull's "IBP's Impact on Lexington, Nebraska: A Report to a Community, June 1, 1996."

The Newcomers

In the middle and late 1980s, new minorities began to show up in southwestern Minnesota in considerable numbers. They came from the small villages, towns, and cities across the world. Most came from southeast Asia, east Africa, and central Mexico and the Texas-Mexico border. Some were victims and political refugees of the Vietnam War and ensuing conflicts. Among the refugees were Hmong, Lao, Cambodians, and Vietnamese. Others came to escape unrest and civil war in east Africa. Yet others moved north along well-trod migration routes out of Texas and Mexico.

We call them new minorities, newcomers, and new residents. Yet, however much we label them as one, there are great differences between and among them. They have different ways, distinct lives, separate pasts, and unique futures.

Their cultures, histories, and migrations put them on varying trajectories. They have been launched by different circumstances and are moved by different desires. They utilize diverse means to follow different paths of migration. Their desire to be at home in this world may be the same, but their migrations are not.

Their families do not take the same form. They marry differently and at different ages. They make different investments in food, clothing, and schooling. Their children arrive in school with differing preparation. On top of this, they have distinct relationships to their homeland: Some will return home; others can never go back.

There are great cultural, class, educational, and regional variations among these immigrants. However, despite great differences, newcomers share one characteristic: They are not at home; home still remains elsewhere for them. Whether they came directly to southwestern Minnesota or arrived after one or more stops along the way, they have a common goal: to find a place to call home, where they can live the good life. This usually means a life that is materially American but culturally similar to what they left behind.

HMONG

The Hmong are one of the many indigenous mountain peoples of southeast Asia. They are part of a larger ethno-linguistic group called Miao, or Meo, that originated in China but was gradually driven south by Chinese expansion. Today the Miao—and the Hmong—live in Laos and northern Vietnam.[1]

Fifty years ago, the Hmong lived in small mountain villages, growing corn, rice, vegetables, and poppies, and keeping pigs and chickens as well as a few draft animals, such as horses and water buffalo. They supplemented their diet by hunting in the jungle. The Hmong were known as fine artisans. Men sometimes worked as blacksmiths, wood carvers, or jewelers, while women worked as weavers and embroiderers. The Hmong did not have a written language until forty years ago. For this reason, story-telling and other oral traditions have played a key role in Hmong life.[2]

By the 1960s, many Hmong were embroiled in the growing conflicts of southeast Asia. Armed and trained with the help of the United States, the Hmong fought a long guerrilla war against communist forces in Laos and Vietnam. Brave and skilled jungle fighters, the Hmong disrupted enemy supply

---

[1]Douglas P. Olney, ed., *A Bibliography of the Hmong (Miao)* (Minneapolis: Center for Urban and Regional Affairs, 1981); *Encyclopedia Americana*, 1994, s.v. "Laos," p. 748.

[2]Wendy Mattison, et al., eds., *Hmong Lives from Laos to La Crosse: Stories of Eight Hmong Elders* (La Crosse: The Pump House, 1994), xix–xxiii; *Encyclopedia Americana*, 1994, s.v. "Laos," p. 748. See also, "Hmong of Minnesota," *Star Tribune*, April 21, 1985, p. 29A–38A; Sarah R. Mason, "The Indochinese: Vietnamese, Ethnic Chinese, Hmong, Lao, Cambodians," in *They Chose Minnesota: A Survey of the State's Ethnic Groups*, June Drenning Holmquist, ed. (St. Paul: Minnesota Historical Society Press, 1981), 586–88.

and communication lines, provided intelligence to the CIA, and rescued downed U.S. fliers. (It is estimated that 100 Hmong lost their lives for every American pilot saved.) Following the American retreat from southeast Asia, the Hmong fought on alone to preserve their independence. Faced with increasing communist reprisals, the Hmong fled their homes for refugee camps in Thailand. Some 50,000 made it to the relative safety of Thailand, with 50,000 more dying along the way due to hunger, disease, dangerous river crossings, and enemy action.[3]

Sponsored by refugee and church groups, with the support of the U.S. government, the Hmong began coming to the United States in the late 1970s. Today, there are large Hmong concentrations in Fresno, California, and St. Paul, Minnesota, as well as in Wisconsin, Michigan, Colorado, and North Carolina.[4]

The first Hmong arrived in southwestern Minnesota in 1991 as part of a plan to relocate them out of the Twin Cities. Many Hmong—traditionally a rural people—were concerned about the effect city life was having on their young people. By the summer of 1991, Heartland Foods in Marshall was employing twenty-four Hmong, most of whom were living in the nearby small village of Lynd, in homes rented from the company.[5]

LAO

The Lao, or Laotian Tai, are the largest single ethnic group in Laos. Like their Hmong neighbors, they left a homeland riven by strife and economic hardship. The Lao migrated from their original homeland in China to southeast Asia in the late thirteenth century. Unlike the Hmong, however, the Lao tend to be a lowland people, inhabiting the Mekong River valley where they grow rice, which forms the staple of their diet.[6]

---

[3]Mattison, et al., *Hmong Lives*, xi–xiii
[4]Ibid., xv.
[5]Les Suzukamo, "Hmong Relocate to New Life in Rural Minnesota," *St. Paul Pioneer Press*, June 30, 1991, p. 1A, 3A.
[6]Mason, "The Indochinese," 588–90.

Like the Vietnamese and other southeast Asian refugees, the Lao began arriving in Minnesota in significant numbers in the late 1970s. By 1981, there were an estimated 2,800 Lao in the state, mostly concentrated in the Twin Cities.[7]

The Lao began arriving in southwestern Minnesota in the 1980s. In 1990, the U.S. census recorded nearly 400 Lao in the nineteen-county southwestern Minnesota region. They have been especially evident in Worthington and Mountain Lake.

Their impact has been most noticeable and welcomed in Mountain Lake, where the arrival of these newcomers has helped the city maintain its schools and revive a depressed housing market. In 1989 a few families arrived, looking for cheap housing. Most had jobs in meatpacking plants elsewhere in the region. These initial "pioneers" paved the way for their compatriots. Within a few years, Mountain Lake was home to fifty-four Lao families, which helped push the city's population back above the 2,000 mark.[8]

VIETNAMESE

Perhaps the first Asian immigrant group to reach southwestern Minnesota in any significant numbers, the Vietnamese began to arrive following the fall of South Vietnam in 1975. They were refugees who had been on the side of the South Vietnamese government during the decades-long Vietnamese War. Most came from that country's Catholic minority and were generally well educated. Some 4,500 came to Minnesota in 1975–76, but quite a few soon left to join family and friends in California and Texas. A new exodus of "boat people" from Vietnam beginning in 1978 brought a steady increase in the number of Vietnamese in the state. In 1980, Minnesota had 7,500 residents of Vietnamese origin (including ethnic Chinese from Vietnam).[9]

The original idea of many church and refugee groups

---

[7]Mason, "The Indochinese," 580.

[8]Lee Egerstrom, "A New Lease on Life: Moving to Rural Areas for Jobs, Asian, African, and Hispanic Immigrant Groups are Rejuvenating Small Minnesota Towns," *St. Paul Pioneer Press*, Jan. 9, 1994, p. 1D.

[9]Mason, "The Indochinese," 580–82.

which sponsored Vietnamese refugees was to distribute the newcomers throughout the region to help spread the burden of assisting them. As a result, nearly every southwestern Minnesota county gained at least some Vietnamese residents during the late 1970s and early 1980s. Most lived in cities such as Willmar, Marshall, or Redwood Falls, but no single county had more than several dozen.

Although this arrangement suited the sponsoring organizations, it did not suit the Vietnamese. The hardships and terrors of escaping from Vietnam, life in the refugee camps, and the bureaucratic nature of the resettlement process left many families separated. Life in the small Minnesota towns left many feeling isolated and adrift in a strange culture. As more family members arrived in America, the refugees sought to bring their scattered kin together. This led most to leave rural Minnesota for larger Vietnamese communities elsewhere in the country. (One of these centers is the Twin Cities, Minneapolis and St. Paul, which has attracted an increasing number of Vietnamese.) Between 1980 and 1990, 263 Vietnamese left southwestern Minnesota. Today, aside from a few individuals, their presence in the region is largely a memory.

SOMALIS

The Somali newcomers, like their east African neighbors the Ethiopians and Sudanese, belong to those many millions of refugees across the globe—16 million in 1994 alone—who fled their homeland to escape persecution, violence, or famine. Somalis are an east African people living primarily in Somalia, but also in parts of Kenya, Djibouti, and Ethiopia. Many are nomads or semi-nomads, while others live in rural villages where they raise livestock and food crops. Most Somalis are Sunni Muslims, and Arabic influences have played an important role in their history. Arabic was the language of writing and education. Aside from Arabic, Somalis had no written language until 1972. Somali culture was based on oral tradition. Somali life is organized around clans and sub-clans, which provide families and individuals with security, protection, and a sense of connection and belonging. Families are the key building blocks of Somali life and provide people with a sense of identity. About 20 percent of all families are polygamous. In cases where men have more than one wife, each wife usually has her own household.[10]

Somalia gained its independence from Italy and Britain by 1960. In 1969, the democratically elected government was overthrown in a socialist coup. In the years that followed, Somalia became a bone of contention in the Cold War conflict between the Soviet Union and the United States, a situation exploited by its increasingly dictatorial ruler, Mohammed Siyaad Barre. In 1991 Siyaad Barre was overthrown as the result of a civil war that had begun in 1988 and split the country along clan and regional lines. The war bred a terrible famine. In 1992, the United States, later supported by the United Nations, sent troops to restore some order and allow food to reach the starving. Although the operation was largely successful, the warring parties failed to reach a peace agreement, and sporadic fighting resumed after the U.N. pullout in February 1995.[11]

Their country's troubles have forced many Somalis to flee their homeland, a movement that has only intensified in the last several years. Many of these refugees are from Somalia's educated class. Although Somalis have come to the United States since the 1920s, and Somali students have been coming to this country since the 1960s, their numbers have remained small. The largest Somali community outside of Africa is in Toronto, Canada, but there are also communities in several major U.S. cities.[12] Somalis, whose main point of entry into the U.S. is California, began arriving in Minnesota in the early 1990s, and some estimate that there are almost 5,000 now living in the state.[13]

The recent Somali immigrants, like their Hmong counterparts, have had their lives and families disrupted by war, the

---

[10]Diana Briton Putnam and Mohamood Cabdi Noor, *The Somalis: Their History and Culture* (Washington, D.C.: Refugee Service Center, Center for Applied Linguistics, 1993), 4–17.

[11]Ibid., 7–13.

[12]Ibid., 1.

[13]Richard Chin, "Somalis Build New Future in Minnesota," *St. Paul Pioneer Press*, March 5, 1995, p. 2B.

refugee camp experience, and demands of the semi-skilled meatpacking jobs many have taken since coming to America. Many Somalis have relatives still living in refugee camps, whom they are trying to support or help to immigrate. As a result of this family fragmentation, many Somali newcomers, accustomed to relying on kin for help and support, have had to rely instead on other, unrelated Somalis who better know the American system and who have better command of some of the basic skills that most Americans take for granted. (For example, few Somali women ever learned to drive while in Somalia, which makes them especially dependent on others for transportation.)

Most Somalis in southwestern Minnesota live in the Marshall area. Many arrived in the summer of 1992 from Sioux Falls and Iowa after the closing of some meatpacking plants there. Prior to coming to the Midwest, many had lived in California. As of 1994, there were an estimated 150 Somalis in Marshall. They make up a significant portion of the work force at Marshall's Heartland Foods. Other Somalis may be found in Worthington. Although most are single males, there are also a growing number of families.[14] Since 1994, some Somalis have migrated out of Marshall, ending up at other meatpacking plants in the region, or in urban centers such as Milwaukee.

In addition to Somalis, the region has played host to other east African peoples who have arrived in smaller numbers. Among them are Kenyans in Marshall, and peoples from Ethiopia in Worthington.

OTHER GROUPS

In addition to the groups listed above, southwestern Minnesota has seen the arrival—and sometimes departure—of several smaller groups of newcomers in the past twenty-five to thirty years. Many have come as students to Southwest State

---

[14]Lutheran Social Services grant application narrative, 1994, in the possession of the authors. In 1994 Somalis made up about a quarter of Heartland's work force. Since then, their numbers seem to have declined, and as of this writing they probably make up about 20 percent of Heartland's workers.

University (SSU—formerly Southwest Minnesota State College) in Marshall. One of the first groups to arrive as students were African Americans in the late 1960s and early 1970s. Neither these incoming students nor the host community were properly prepared, resulting in numerous misunderstandings and a few confrontations. The majority of the African American students left after a short period of time, although a few stayed on. Smaller numbers of African American students have continued to enroll at SSU over the years.[15]

SSU has also brought a small but steady stream of foreign students to the region. In the late 1970s and 1980s, the school had a fair number of students from the Middle East, primarily Iranians and Palestinians. This proved especially tense when America's involvement in the Middle East was frequently fraught with tragedy and drama.

More recently, the Marshall area has been host to about a dozen Kenyans and a few people from Cameroon. The region has also seen the arrival of persons from eastern Europe and the former Soviet Union. Some have come as students, others to settle.

MEXICANS, MEXICAN AMERICANS, AND OTHER LATINO GROUPS

Mexicans are America's oldest and newest immigrants. They are descendants of Spanish and other European settlers and native peoples. The ancestors of some Mexicans lived in what is today the continental United States before the nation existed. Large portions of Mexican territory were annexed or purchased by the United States in the nineteenth century. The Mexicans living in those lands became U.S. subjects by default. Since the late nineteenth century, but particularly after 1910, Mexicans have also been coming to the U.S. to work in the fields and mines of the West and Southwest. Many came only

[15]See Joseph Amato and John Radzilowski, *A New College on the Prairie: Twenty-Five Years of Southwest State University* (Marshall, Minn.: Crossings Press, 1992), 46–47.

temporarily to earn some extra money, but others settled and stayed.[16]

Immigration from Mexico increased dramatically in the 1920s. This resulted from severe restrictions placed on "undesirable" immigrants from eastern and southern Europe. Although Mexicans were viewed as no more "desirable" than Greeks, Italians, or Poles, a powerful agricultural lobby made up of growers from the West and Southwest, who wanted cheap farm labor, managed to get Mexicans exempted from the immigration-restriction legislation of the 1920s. As a result, Mexicans not only entered the country to work in farm fields in the Southwest, but also came to the Midwest and Great Lakes region to work in agriculture and industry. In addition to field work, Mexicans found jobs in the meatpacking, railroad, and steel industries.[17]

During the 1920s, Mexicans and Mexican Americans came to Minnesota in significant numbers. The 1930 census listed 3,626 Mexicans in the state. Although the largest community was in St. Paul, most were in rural areas, and there were a surprising number in the nineteen counties of southwestern Minnesota.[18] A small community of several families lived and worked at a small tile-making plant in Marshall in the 1920s.

---

[16]For works on the history of Mexican Americans, see Rodolfo Acuña, *Occupied America: A History of Chicanos*, 3d ed. (New York: Harper and Row, 1988); Stan Steiner, *La Raza: The Mexican Americans* (New York: Harper and Row, 1970); Allen Englekirk and Marguerite Marín, "Mexican Americans," *Gale Encyclopedia of Multicultural America*, Rudolph J. Vecoli, ed. (New York: Gale Research Inc., 1995), 2:905–39.

[17]Acuña, *Occupied America*, 128–30; Englekirk and Marín, "Mexican Americans," 907–8.

[18]Susan M. Diebold, "Mexicans," in *They Chose Minnesota: A Survey of the State's Ethnic Groups* (St. Paul: Minnesota Historical Society Press, 1981), 93–94.

TABLE 1

Mexicans and Hispanics in Southwestern Minnesota, 1930, 1970, and 1990[19]

COUNTY	Foreign Born (census indication) 1930	Spanish Mother Tongue (census indication) 1970	Mexican and Mexican-American Ancestry (census indication) 1990
Brown	8	47	127
Chippewa	11	36	63
Cottonwood	0	16	35
Jackson	90	7	58
Kandiyohi	91	83	1,016
Lincoln	0	8	9
Lyon	0	95	184
Martin	245	5	79
Murray	0	94	9
Nobles	276	105	344
Redwood	11	7	33
Renville	88	14	205
Watonwan	20	20	524
Yellow Medicine	97	5	55
TOTALS	937	542	2,741

The number of Mexicans living year-round in the region in the 1920s was probably small. Most came for the summer and then returned to the Twin Cities, or perhaps to Texas or Mexico, for the winter. Whole families came to work, usually earning less than $350 a season.[20]

During the Depression, American nativism focused on Mexicans. Many Mexicans, including many who were U.S. citizens, were deported. Between 300,000 and 500,000 people were removed from their homes and sent to Mexico.[21] As the U.S. entered World War II, however, it suddenly found itself

[19]Ibid., 94, and 1990 Bureau of the Census, ancestry figures.
[20]Ibid., 95.
[21]Acuña, *Occupied America*, 138.

short of labor. Thus was born the "Bracero" program, which brought Mexican workers northward once again to work in American fields. Although it was supposed to be a temporary measure, powerful agricultural interests convinced Congress to keep the program going after the war. The Bracero program lasted until 1964.[22] Most Mexican laborers who came to Minnesota in this era worked in the Red River Valley. The 1960 census turned up almost no Mexicans in southwestern Minnesota.[23]

Since the late 1960s, the number of Mexicans in the region has steadily increased, with more dramatic increases occurring in the last several years. This new wave of migration consists of two groups. Mexicans coming directly from Mexico and who may be in the United States either legally or illegally make up about 30–40 percent of all persons of Mexican ancestry in the area. The second and larger group is made up of Mexican Americans. They come primarily from the Texas-Mexico border, which is defined by the Rio Grande, stretching from El Paso/Ciudad Juárez, to Eagle Pass/Piedras Negras, to Brownsville/Matamoros. To outsiders, the differences between the two groups are not readily apparent, for both share much in terms of culture and language. (These two groups are often referred to as "Chicanos." People of Latin American origin are sometimes known as Latinos, or, by government definition, Hispanics. How they refer to themselves is a more complex matter, with many Mexicans shunning a primary national identity.)

The movement of Mexicans and other Latinos to southwestern Minnesota is part of a larger Latino movement to the upper midwestern states that has been occurring in fits and starts since the 1920s, but which has accelerated in recent decades. Illinois—particularly Chicago—has received the largest number of new Latinos, about 1 million by 1990, but all other states in the region have also seen an increase in the Latino

---

[22]Ibid., 144–50.

[23]Diebold, "Mexicans," 94.

population.[24] Currently, Hispanics are the eighteenth largest ethnic group in Minnesota with 53,884 people, according to the 1990 census.[25]

Although Mexicans and Mexican Americans still come to this region as farm laborers (and they now work jobs far beyond the area's sugar beet fields), Mexicans and Mexican Americans now find work in regional meatpacking plants. Of all the newcomers to southwestern Minnesota, Mexicans and Mexican Americans have provided the largest and most consistent source of labor for the meatpacking industry.

Small numbers of other Hispanic groups, including Guatemalans, Salvadorans, and Cubans, have also migrated to southwestern Minnesota. In addition, some recent immigrants from southern Mexico are Indians for whom Spanish is a second language.

The largest and oldest Hispanic concentration in southwestern Minnesota is in Willmar, which had over 1,000 residents of Mexican ancestry by 1990. Other towns with significant concentrations are St. James, Worthington, Olivia, and Marshall. In addition to the primary migration links to south Texas and Mexico, these communities have also begun to develop ties to the larger Mexican community in the Twin Cities. This is especially true of the smaller numbers of Mexicans who have made rural Minnesota their home since the 1970s.

Meatpacking and farm labor continue to provide the majority of jobs that draw Mexicans and other Latinos to southwestern Minnesota, both for temporary and long-term migrants. Yet, a small number have begun to find work in other industries as well, as evidenced by the small number of Mexicans appearing in areas relatively distant from meatpacking plants. Whether this trend continues and whether Latinos become permanent residents in the region remains to be seen.

---

[24]Robert Aponte and Marcelo Siles, "Latinos in the Heartland: The Browning of the Midwest," Julian Samora Research Institute, research report 5, Nov. 1994, Figures 2–3.

[25]This counts all Hispanic groups. Some Latino leaders in Minnesota have challenged these numbers.

Counting the Newcomers

Newcomers go where there are jobs and housing. Asians have often come with the aid of church groups. Mexicans and Mexican Americans stay in areas they are familiar with due to previous migration cycles.

Their arrival in truly significant numbers is a recent event. As late as 1990, southwestern Minnesota still recorded an insignificant foreign-born population. Indeed, the high rate of mortality among the older European immigrants and a continuing shift of rural peoples to urban centers caused an approximately 50 percent decline in the number of foreign born in southwestern Minnesota in the 1970s and 1980s. In the same period, only Jackson and Nobles counties underwent a growth in their foreign-born population, while the five counties at the heart of this study (Cottonwood, Jackson, Nobles, Lyon, and Watonwan) experienced a 5.81 percent decline in their total population. But significant numbers of foreign born have been arriving since 1990.

The percentage of officially defined minorities, including blacks and American Indians, grew to 5.6 percent of the state's population, up from 3.4 percent in 1980. Of course, the largest increase occurred in the Twin Cities, with its growing black population and its relatively concentrated Asian populations. Of the 300,000 people the state added, 22,000 were Hispanic, and 100,000 were black, Asian, and American Indian. The state's American Indian population grew 43 percent to 50,000; the black population grew 78 percent to 94,000. The Asian population jumped by 194 percent. Hispanic organizations estimated their population at 69,000 in 1990.

By the 1980s, these minorities assumed greater visibility in southwestern Minnesota as they concentrated in small villages, towns, and cities where poultry, food-processing, and electronics were expanding and establishing themselves. Their arrival came at a time of farm and small business loss and population decline. This multifaceted regional decline—the subject of the book *The Decline of Rural Minnesota*—made the appearance of these newcomers a matter of hope and encouragement.[1] Lee Egerstrom of the *St. Paul Pioneer Press* was not alone in seeing the arrival of the Hmong in Mountain Lake as a source of hope for regional renewal. The new Asian, African, and Hispanic populations awoke similar hopes in other communities.

Their arrival is represented by the following tables. Our projections are based on population estimates from the state demographer and school attendance data. To integrate these data we used a regression forecast model that combines and averages estimates from 1980 to 1990, and 1990 to 1994, with school data from 1990 to 1995. More complex considerations would require weighing such factors as the high fertility of the newcomers; likely industrial expansion and decline; the degree to which newcomers will fill industrial positions; and the rate at which minorities will diffuse into the region's general labor force or leave the area. With this said, we offer the following tables and graphs with the warning that no matter how clever the wizardry of hypothesis and conjecture, the picture for 2000 remains a speculative affair.

[1]Joseph Amato and John Meyer, *The Decline of Rural Minnesota* (Marshall, Minn.: Crossings Press, 1993).

Tables of Race–Ethnicity Population Trends, Estimates and Forecast for Five-County Study Area

TABLE 2

Total Population Estimate and Forecast
Five-County Study Area

COUNTY	1980	1990	1995	2000
Lyon	25,207	24,789	24,938	25,088
Nobles	21,840	20,096	19,816	19,539
Jackson	13,690	11,677	11,149	10,622
Cottonwood	14,854	12,694	12,178	11,661
Watonwan	12,361	11,682	11,471	11,267

TABLE 3

White Population Estimate and Forecast
Five-County Study Area

COUNTY	1980	1990	1995	2000
Lyon	24,920	24,401	23,596	23,676
Nobles	21,583	19,400	17,339	16,766
Jackson	13,625	11,414	10,750	10,114
Cottonwood	14,785	12,563	11,272	10,683
Watonwan	12,185	11,120	10,042	10,055

TABLE 4

White Population as a Percent of the Total Population
Five-County Study Area

COUNTY	1980	1990	1995	2000
Lyon	98.86%	98.43%	94.62%	94.37%
Nobles	98.82%	96.54%	87.50%	85.81%
Jackson	99.53%	97.75%	96.42%	95.22%
Cottonwood	99.54%	98.97%	92.56%	91.61%
Watonwan	98.58%	95.19%	87.54%	89.24%

TABLE 5

Minority Population Estimate and Forecast Five-County Study Area

COUNTY	1980	1990	1995	2000
Lyon	287	388	1,342	1,412
Nobles	257	696	2,477	2,773
Jackson	65	263	399	508
Cottonwood	69	131	906	978
Watonwan	176	562	1,429	1,212

TABLE 6

Minority Population as a Percent of the Total Population Five-County Study Area

COUNTY	1980	1990	1995	2000
Lyon	1.14%	1.57%	5.38%	5.63%
Nobles	1.18%	3.46%	12.50%	14.19%
Jackson	0.47%	2.25%	3.58%	4.78%
Cottonwood	0.46%	1.03%	7.44%	8.39%
Watonwan	1.42%	4.81%	12.46%	10.76%

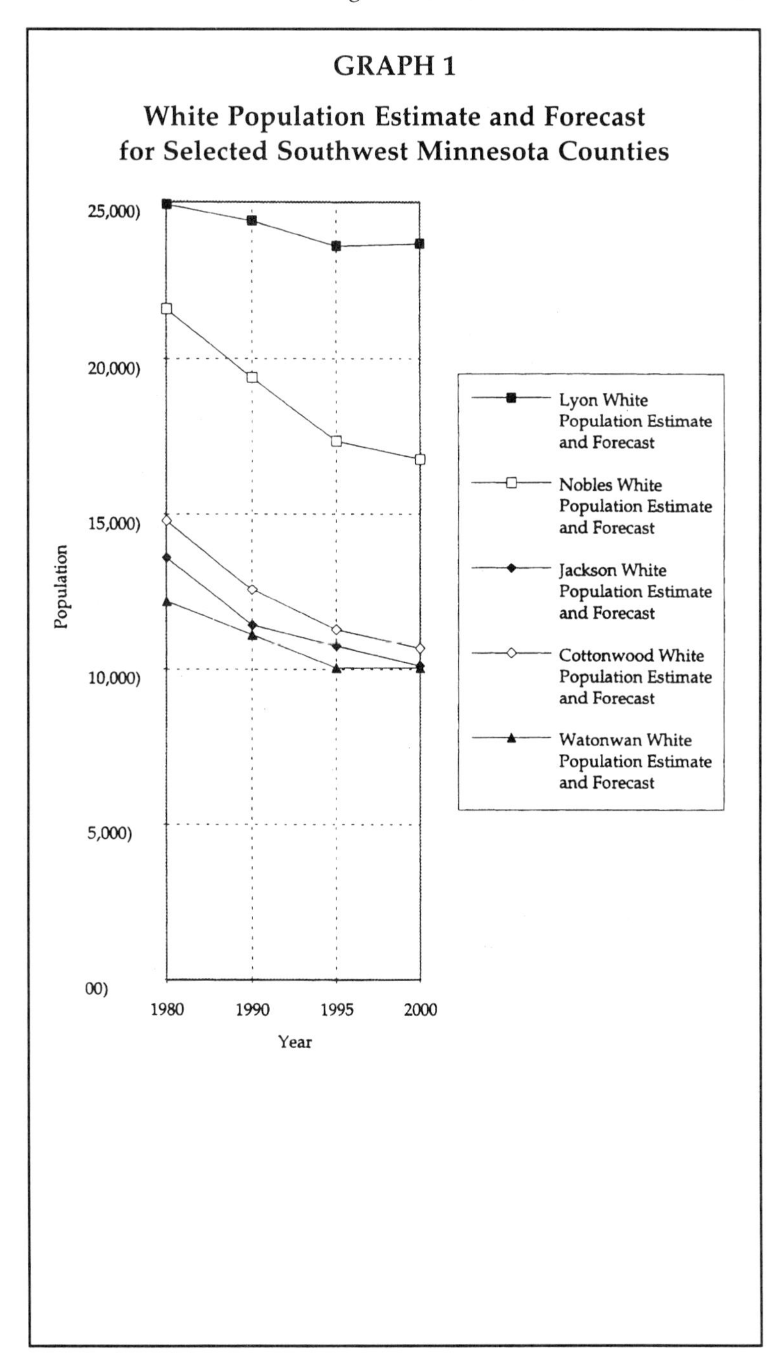
GRAPH 1
White Population Estimate and Forecast for Selected Southwest Minnesota Counties
25,000)
20,000)
15,000)
10,000)
5,000)
00)
Population
1980
1990
1995
2000
Year
Lyon White Population Estimate and Forecast
Nobles White Population Estimate and Forecast
Jackson White Population Estimate and Forecast
Cottonwood White Population Estimate and Forecast
Watonwan White Population Estimate and Forecast

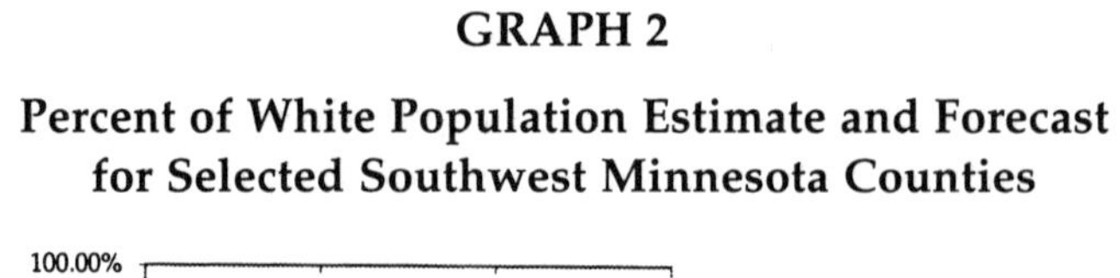

GRAPH 2

Percent of White Population Estimate and Forecast for Selected Southwest Minnesota Counties

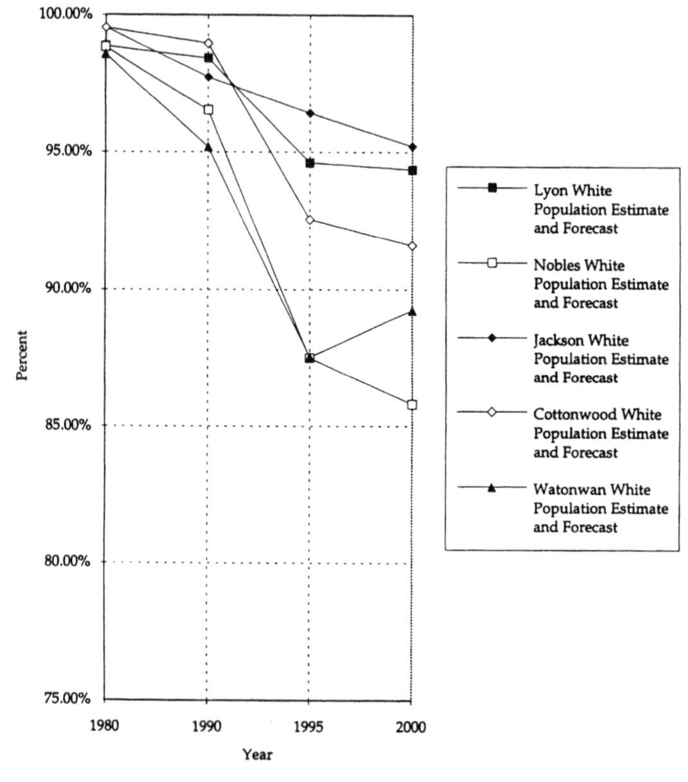

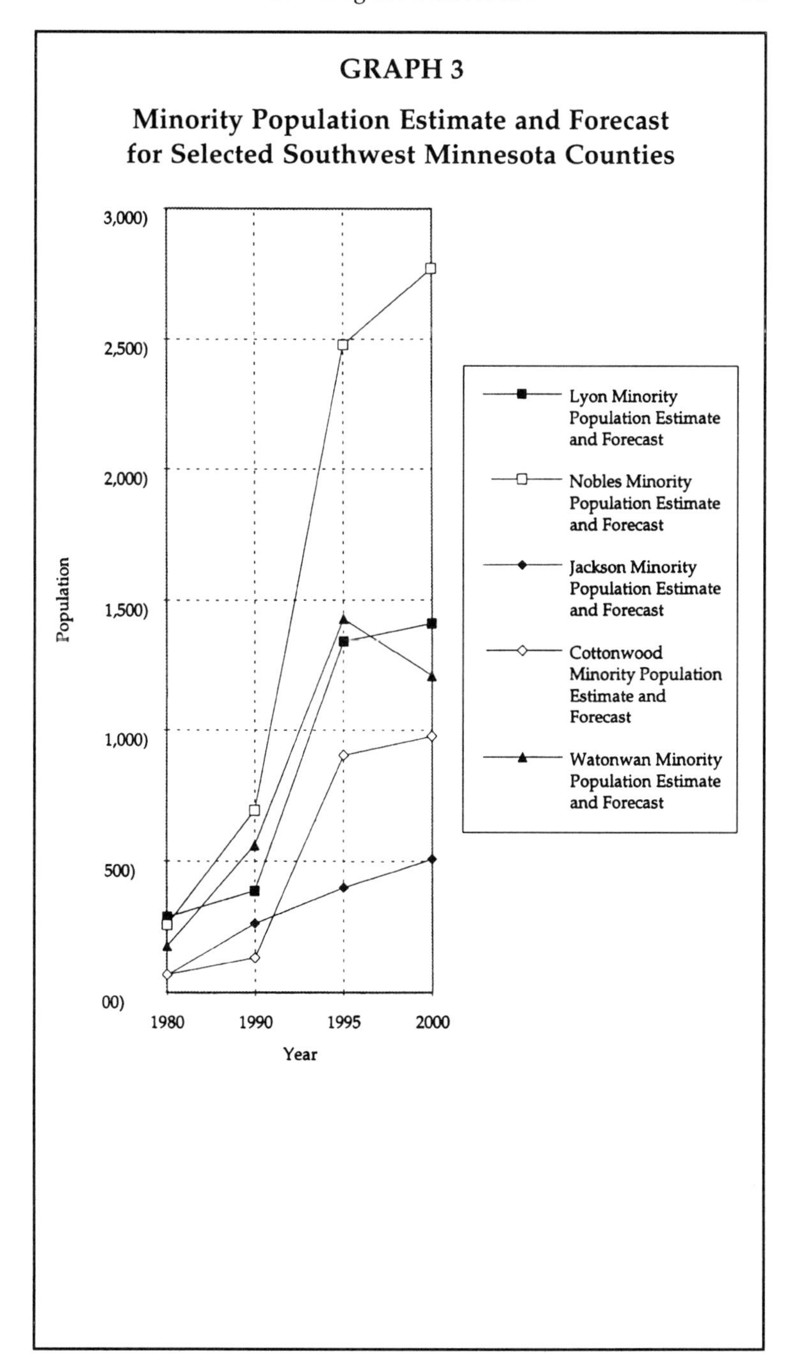
GRAPH 3
Minority Population Estimate and Forecast for Selected Southwest Minnesota Counties
3,000)
2,500)
2,000)
1,500)
1,000)
500)
00)
Population
1980
1990
1995
2000
Year
Lyon Minority Population Estimate and Forecast
Nobles Minority Population Estimate and Forecast
Jackson Minority Population Estimate and Forecast
Cottonwood Minority Population Estimate and Forecast
Watonwan Minority Population Estimate and Forecast

GRAPH 4

Percent of Minority Population Estimate and Forecast for Selected Southwest Minnesota Counties

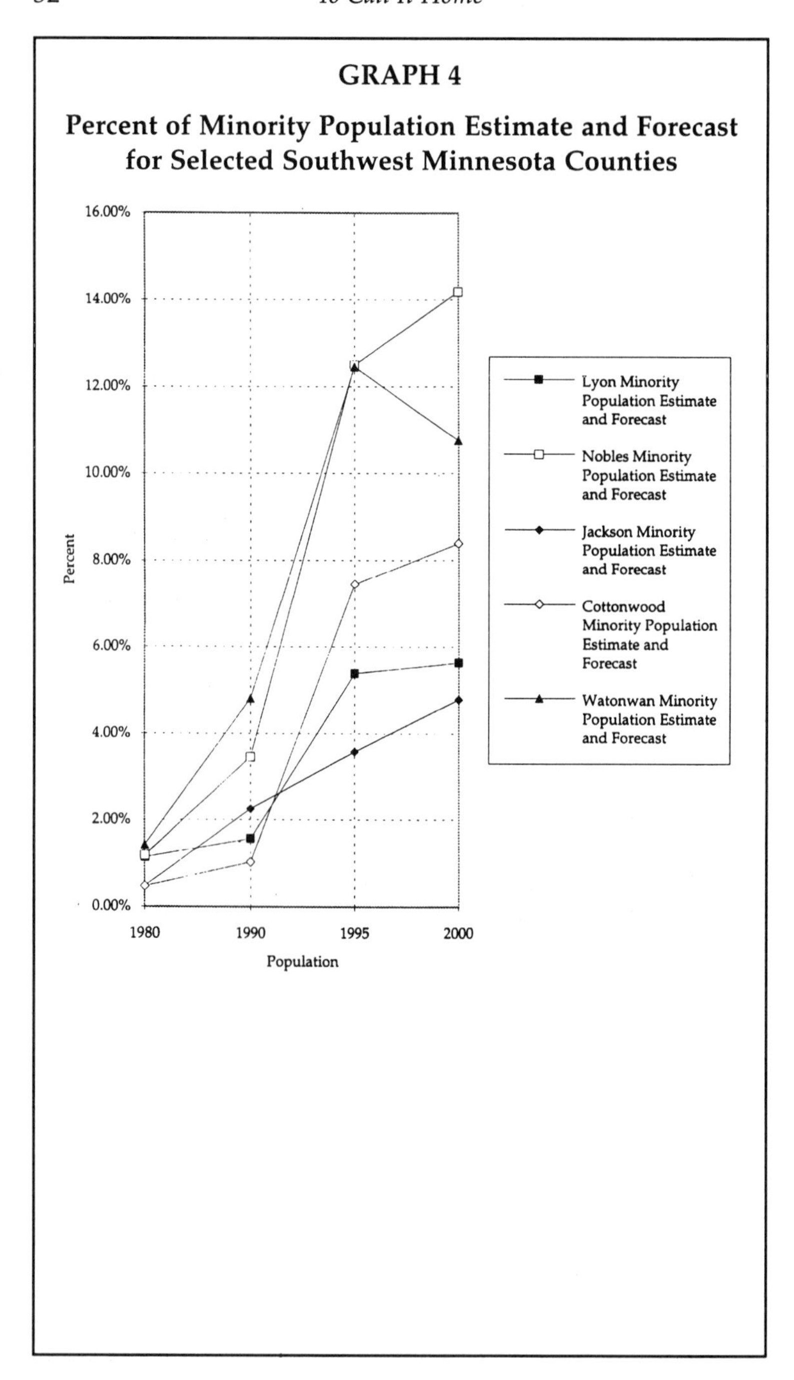

Tables of Race–Ethnicity Population Trends, Estimates and Forecast for Selected Cities in Southwest Minnesota

TABLE 7

White Population Estimate and Forecast for Selected Cities in Southwest Minnesota

CITY	1980	1990	1995	2000
Marshall	10,922	11,740	11,473	12,173
Worthington	10,032	9,343	8,169	7,750
St. James	4,262	4,078	3,652	3,618
Tracy	2,449	2,033	1,842	1,622
Mountain Lake	2,264	1,831	1,517	1,456
Madelia	2,054	2,052	1,927	1,892

TABLE 8

White Population Percent Estimate and Forecast for Selected Cities in Southwest Minnesota

CITY	1980	1990	1995	2000
Marshall	97.86%	97.45%	91.99%	94.09%
Worthington	97.94%	93.65%	81.28%	77.44%
St. James	98.07%	93.45%	83.82%	83.08%
Tracy	98.83%	98.74%	89.74%	88.55%
Mountain Lake	99.43%	96.07%	83.82%	84.90%
Madelia	96.43%	91.73%	85.24%	82.71%

TABLE 9

Minority Population Estimate and Forecast for Selected Cities in Southwest Minnesota

CITY	1980	1990	1995	2000
Marshall	239	283	999	765
Worthington	209	634	1,881	2,258
St. James	84	286	705	737
Tracy	29	26	211	210
Mountain Lake	13	75	293	259
Madelia	76	185	334	396

TABLE 10

Minority Population Percent Estimate and Forecast for Selected Cities in Southwest Minnesota

CITY	1980	1990	1995	2000
Marshall	2.14%	2.55%	8.01%	5.91%
Worthington	2.06%	6.35%	18.72%	22.56%
St. James	1.93%	6.55%	16.18%	16.92%
Tracy	1.17%	1.26%	10.26%	11.45%
Mountain Lake	0.57%	3.93%	16.18%	15.10%
Madelia	3.57%	8.27%	14.76%	17.29%

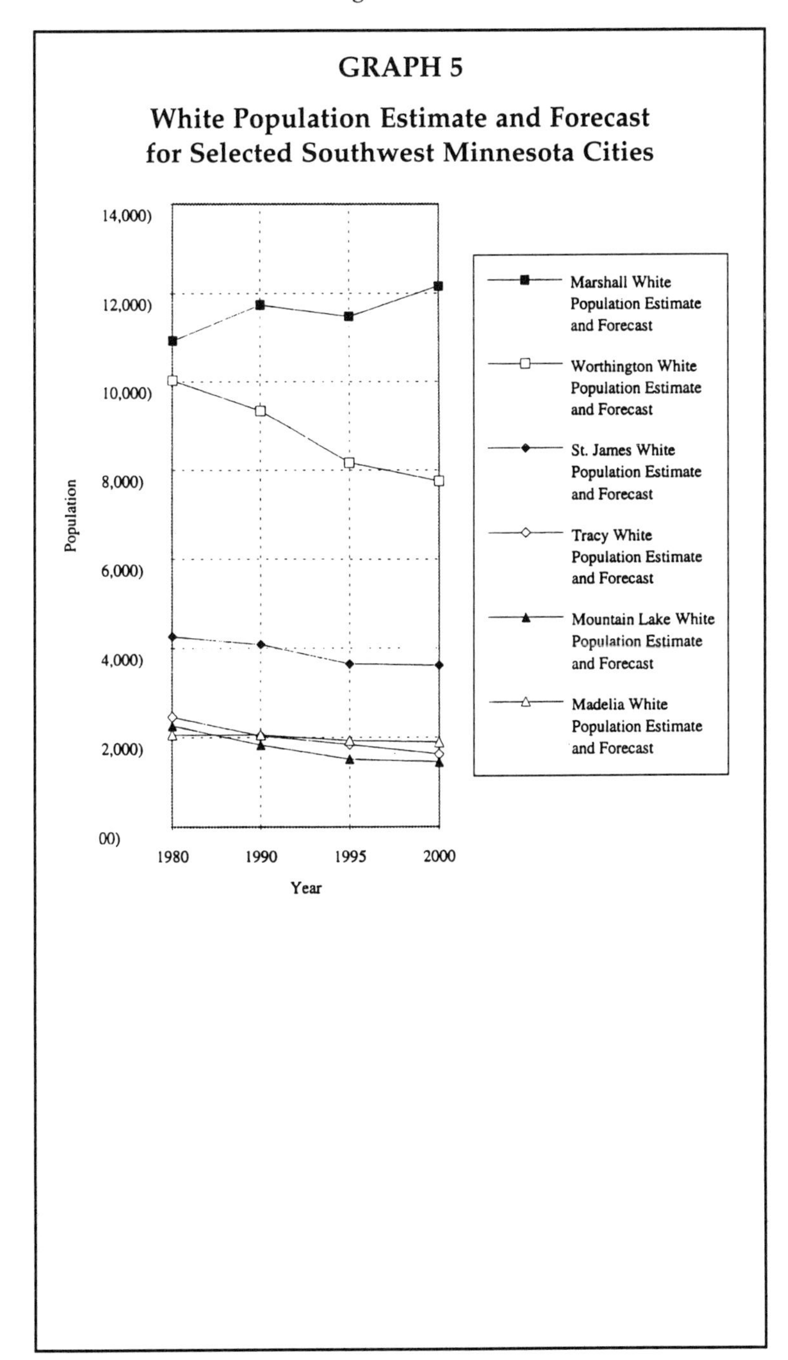

GRAPH 5
White Population Estimate and Forecast for Selected Southwest Minnesota Cities
14,000)
12,000)
10,000)
8,000)
6,000)
4,000)
2,000)
00)
Population
1980
1990
1995
2000
Year
Marshall White Population Estimate and Forecast
Worthington White Population Estimate and Forecast
St. James White Population Estimate and Forecast
Tracy White Population Estimate and Forecast
Mountain Lake White Population Estimate and Forecast
Madelia White Population Estimate and Forecast

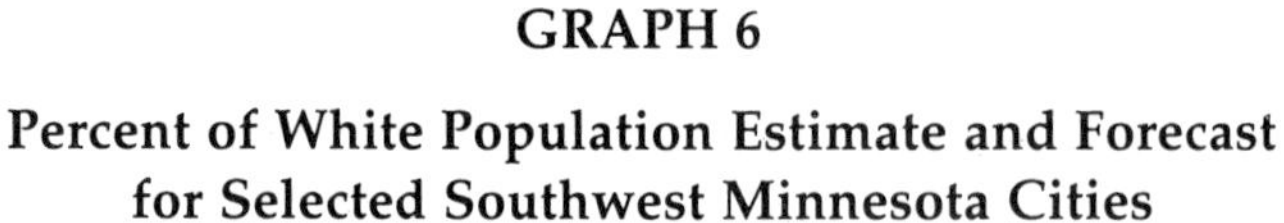

GRAPH 6

Percent of White Population Estimate and Forecast for Selected Southwest Minnesota Cities

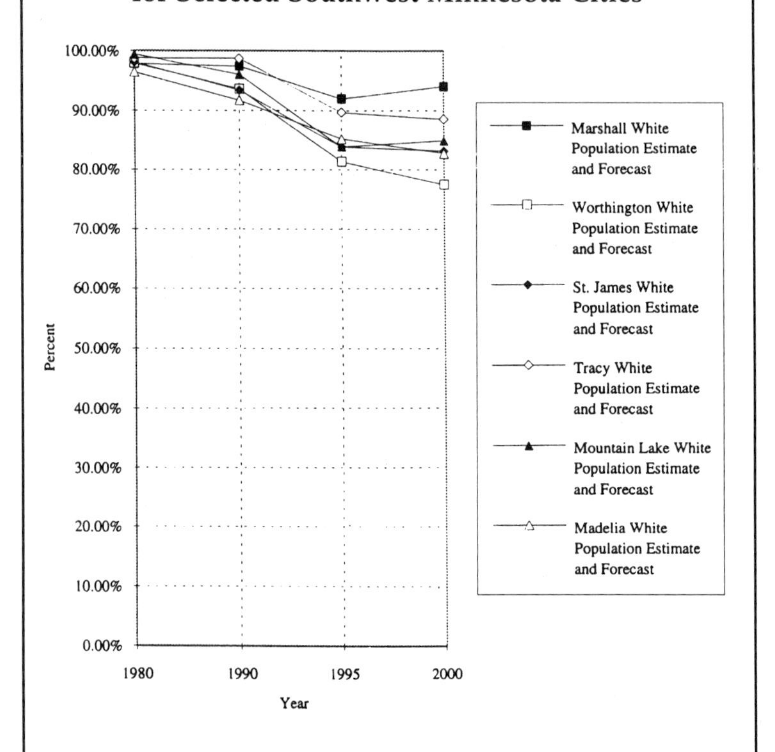

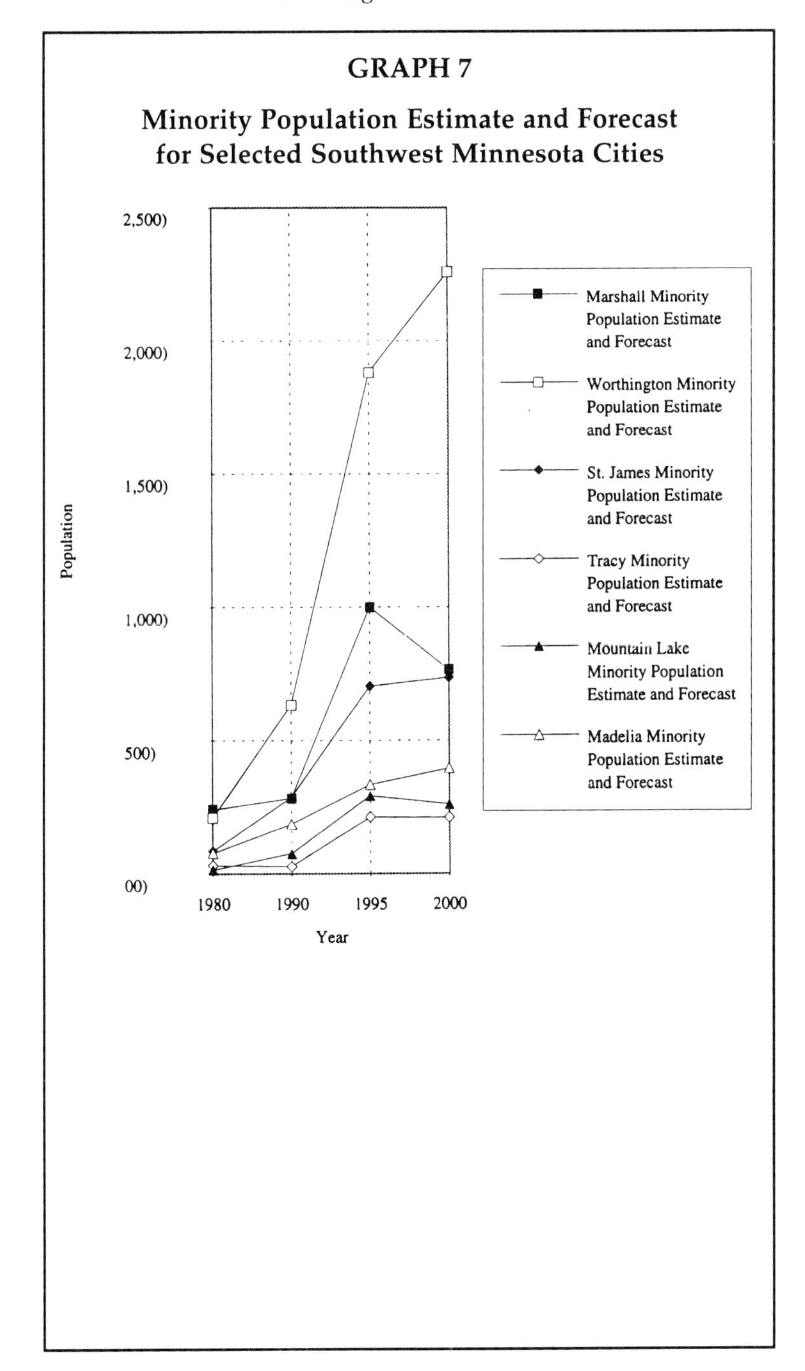
GRAPH 7
Minority Population Estimate and Forecast
for Selected Southwest Minnesota Cities
2,500)
2,000)
1,500)
1,000)
500)
00)
Population
1980
1990
1995
2000
Year
Marshall Minority Population Estimate and Forecast
Worthington Minority Population Estimate and Forecast
St. James Minority Population Estimate and Forecast
Tracy Minority Population Estimate and Forecast
Mountain Lake Minority Population Estimate and Forecast
Madelia Minority Population Estimate and Forecast

GRAPH 8

Percent of Minority Population Estimate and Forecast for Selected Southwest Minnesota Cities

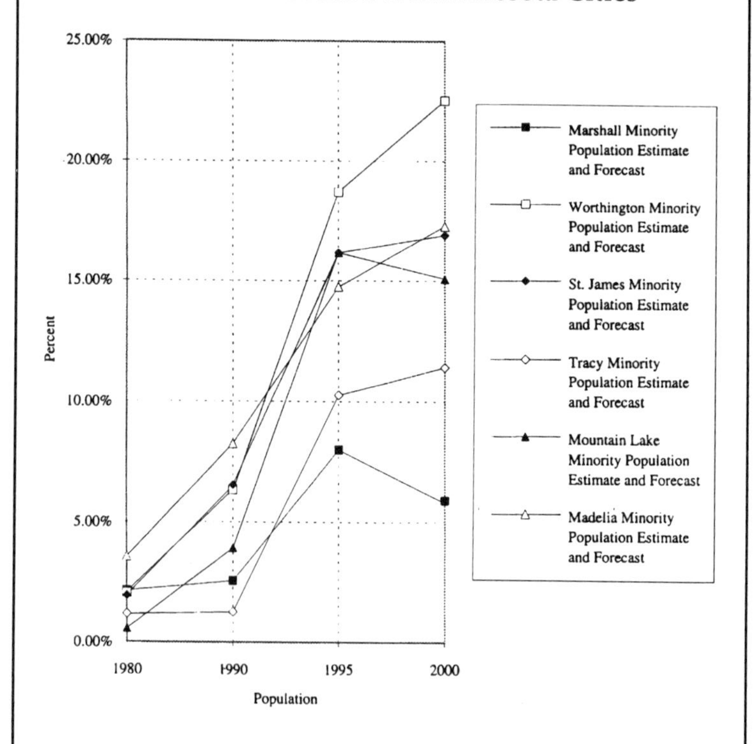

Birds of a Feather

The story of minorities in southwestern Minnesota is part of the story of the region's new and expanding meat- and particularly poultry-processing industry. Although this overlooks a smaller industry of electronic processing and other employers, the presence of newcomers in southwestern Minnesota, as well as their conditions and their future in the region, turns on the motives, actions, and fortunes of the poultry industry.

The poultry and pork industries determine where newcomers are located in the region: Marshall, Worthington, Willmar, St. James, Madelia, and Montevideo. Throughout the nation, the rapidly expanding poultry industry—similar to beef, pork, and fish industries—has gone to the countryside where there is less profit lost to transportation and spoilage, where unions are weak or non-existent, and where cheap labor exists or can be brought in cheaply. Indeed, the $3 billion industry has been increasingly ruralized.[1]

Due to technological innovations, corporate restructuring, the weakening of unions, and the assumption that it is cheaper to bring workers to their rural sites rather than unprocessed birds to the cities, the industry has drawn the newest and poorest in the nation to its service.[2] The ruralization of the industry was reinforced in the 1980s as towns, desperate to pre-

---

[1]Joe Rigert and Richard Meryhew, "In the Meat Factories," *Star Tribune*, April 30, 1995, 1A, 11A–13A.

[2]Michael J. Broadway, "From City to Countryside: Recent Changes in the Structure and Location of the Meat- and Fish-Processing Industries," in *Any Way You Cut It: Meat Processing and Small-Town America*, Donald D. Stull, et al., eds. (Lawrence: University Press of Kansas, 1995), 17–40.

serve or create jobs at any cost, provided meat-processing industries with tax breaks and other incentives. In return, the towns got jobs, but at low wages, and under such strenuous conditions that most host community residents would not take them (a high school diploma and a minimal vocational education is enough to get employment beyond the cutting floor). To get the workers they need, companies must look elsewhere for labor, and, invariably, they look to newer and poorer Americans. Work in the meat-processing industry is almost always available, it requires only minimal English, and for immigrants from low-wage economies, the $6- to $7-an-hour starting wage is good money. This is why Hispanics, southeast Asians, and east Africans have been drawn to the packing houses in the region.

Mexicans and Mexican Americans have been the industry's workhorses. They have continued to fuel the industry and been tough enough to stay with it, as poor European Americans (the old core of the labor force) steadily exit and other new immigrants leave it as opportunities permit. The industry has found its greatest source of Latino workers along both sides of the 1,200-mile border between Texas and Mexico—*la frontera*—formed by the Rio Grande.

Like American agriculture, the new industry found along *la frontera* a poor, hard-working people long conditioned to traveling north. Composed of both long-time residents of U.S. and Mexican bordertowns and newly arrived Mexicans from the impoverished *ranchitos* of central Mexico, these people see the north as a chance to improve their condition. Like earlier immigrants from eastern and southern Europe who came to work in the Midwest's slaughterhouses and packing plants, Latino workers follow family and friends who have gone on ahead; they are willing to make tremendous personal sacrifices to better their economic conditions, to save up enough money for a home, and to make a better life for their children.

The meat-processing industry rises and falls with its ability to bring these people north. Its whole philosophy of the 1980s, of deunionization, of lower wages and greater productivity, turns on its ability to attract these workers to distant rural cities.

By paying a $6-plus-an-hour starting wage—having paid almost $12-an-hour average wage a decade earlier, before deunionization—with approximately a 25 percent accident rate (it was 28 percent in 1990 for poultry processing) and annual turnover rates between 50 and 80 percent, the industry determines the lives of its workers and shapes the city where it exists. With full employment, no accidents or sickness, a new worker (at $6 an hour) will earn $12,000 for a fifty-week work year, $3,000 short of the federal poverty line. Along with this starting wage comes unsafe, overcrowded, and inferior housing, and little or no margin for savings. An accident or a layoff can crush the fragile dream of getting ahead. For workers, particularly Latinos, who come to this region's poultry- and pork-processing plants, their jobs and the decision to migrate involve a series of difficult trade-offs and gambles. On one hand they must accept dirty, difficult, and dangerous jobs; on the other, the jobs they could have had at home were hardly less strenuous. They must leave a familiar place and journey to a foreign land. They must gamble that their new and improved wages will provide their families with a living, that they will not be injured, and that just possibly over the years they can save up enough for a house. Those who succeed move from the ranks of the poor into the ranks of the working class. Those for whom the gamble does not pay off face welfare, return to an even more impoverished hometown, social dislocation, even tragedy. In any case, a family's luck, discipline, and capacity for shared sacrifice—not generous wages—will determine the outcome of their migration. Whether the newcomers achieve the stability and security they desire has much to do with whether they will become permanent, productive citizens here, and whether they decide to call this region home.

To Help or To Hate?

Local leaders know and can count on certain things. On the positive side, they can be sure that state and county agencies will provide a wide range of services. At the same time, certain groups may be eligible for special state and federal programs and all may experience special help from local government and industry for settling in, housing, and education. With varying degrees of enthusiasm and imagination, and not necessarily in any predictable order, social services, the police, and educators will adjust attitudes, practice fairness, and meet particular needs of newcomers. The best governmental efforts will be augmented by acts of hospitality, generosity, and charity on the part of host churches and other voluntary organizations. By any measure, today's newcomers are provided with more services than immigrants in any past period in history. (See appendix for a list of services available to newcomers and others.) Although there are legally mandated services available to all groups, newcomers may also avail themselves of informal assistance.

On a completely informal basis, many communities have devised ways to help new arrivals. Most police departments will provide $5 or $10 for gas, provide a night's lodging at a motel, and the cost of a meal. Most churches will do the same. Some parishes have special funds set aside to help those in need. Holy Redeemer Catholic Church in Marshall has a "Partners in Justice" fund, and St. John Vianney Catholic Church in Fairmont has a "Good Samaritan Fund." The Church of St. James in St. James maintains a used clothing center, which also gives out bedding and diapers. The center will also provide help in paying power, gas, and food bills on an emergency basis. "We just want them to know we care," says Fr. Richard Riordan.

Both the Winona and the New Ulm diocese have offices of Hispanic ministry. Many parishes in both dioceses have Spanish masses on a regular basis. In Marshall, a Spanish mass is scheduled every Sunday, as are adult Bible studies and religious education for children. Several parishes celebrate feast days significant to Mexican people. *La Posada* (procession of Jesus and Mary) is held at Christmas time, and the feast of Our Lady of Guadalupe (December 12) is celebrated with a special mass, a potluck supper, and *piñatas* for the children. On Good Friday, the Mexican tradition of following the Way of the Cross outdoors is honored. When a girl reaches her fifteenth birthday, her *quinceañera* is celebrated with a special mass. Holy Redeemer parish also offers income tax preparation assistance.

The Lao Family Community in Marshall assists that ethnic group by providing interpreters, helping Laotians find jobs and housing, and directing them to available assistance. The Laotian community in Mountain Lake has formed its own Christian congregation led by Pastor Tong Chitchalerntham, who is also available as a translator. The community also has a Laotian task force composed of people from Mountain Lake and surrounding towns that meets monthly to discuss the Laotians' needs and to provide help with housing, job placement, and even household goods.

Lutheran Social Services of Marshall placed Jonathan Harris and then Ruth Saad El-Dein in charge of its program to help Somali refugees. The program is funded through a federal grant to communities experiencing an unexpected influx of refugees. It is meant to find jobs for the new immigrants. It also makes translators available and offers employment training and counseling. Young parents are taught parenting skills and given nutrition education. The purpose of the program is to educate both Somalis and the host community in mutual acceptance, understanding, and respect, and to link them as members of one community.

In July 1994, Minnesota Advocates for Human Rights met

with Marshall community leaders as part of the B.I.A.S. Project (Building Immigrant Awareness and Support) which was funded by the Bremer Foundation to counter anti-immigrant sentiment in Minnesota. One of the needs that surfaced was for the community to receive more education on the history of regional immigration. A short-term solution was offered to get a booth at the Lyon County Fair to celebrate the continuum of immigrant groups—both past and present—who have settled in Lyon County. A small group formed to take on this project and named themselves "People for Community Harmony" (PCH). People for Community Harmony continued to meet monthly and formed committees such as housing, health care, education, communication, and special events. People for Community Harmony disbanded in the spring of 1995. In its short existence, perhaps the most notable accomplishment was the support network it created between people working with immigrants in different areas of the community.

In Tracy, the city has established a revolving fund to help newcomers buy homes. A summer picnic at Garvin Park drew over 200 Hmong from throughout the area. Mayor John Almlie addressed the gathering. When fire took the lives of two Mexican children in 1993, many Tracy residents came to the aid of the bereaved family. The mayor, who is also the funeral director, was one of the men who went into the grave to receive the casket as is the custom of the Mexican people.

Worthington hosts an International Festival in July featuring ethnic music, cuisine, and soccer. The southeast Asian population sponsors an Asian New Year celebration to which the entire community is invited.

St. James has introduced soccer into its school athletics and has hired a soccer coach to encourage the participation of the newcomers in school athletics. The St. James newspaper, the *Plainsdealer*, has introduced a special feature for its Spanish-speaking readers, "Cultura Hispanica" (Hispanic Culture). This section features articles on Hispanic culture in both English and Spanish. It is the editor's way of trying to bring the two communities together.

Shirley Anderson-Porisch, Lyon County Extension educator, notes that the host community is beginning to cater to newcomers. Grocery stores, for example, are beginning to carry more Mexican and Asian foods. Anderson-Porisch sees this as a sign of the community's acceptance of newcomers.

The lack of translators for those who do not speak English is one of the major barriers to newcomers' full participation in work and society. Translators may be found in schools (where they are often more important to establishing rapport between the school and the parents than they are to the children), the courts, doctors' offices, and government offices, to name a few. There are many ways the host communities are trying to assist the newcomers and make them feel at home. All avenues for assistance have not been explored or exhausted, but these efforts are a good beginning.

At the same time, leaders must recognize that newcomers will encounter prejudice, stereotypes and, at times, overt racism. It will come in the form of a shopkeeper who insists on shadowing them to make sure they don't steal something, the clerk challenging their truthfulness, or the courthouse worker accusing them of special privilege or advantage. It may take the form of ordinances making English the official language, or new housing ordinances forbidding any new trailer park sites. Yet it can manifest itself in blaming the newcomers for making a place unsafe and the schools violent.

Distrust, resentment, and even anger are here, waiting for the newcomers. They come from long-standing nativism and racism. They are fed by national debates over welfare, affirmative action, and English as an official language. Recently, they have been sparked by anti-immigration feeling, criticism of government programs, fear of crime, and accusations that our nation fails its own working classes.

Dark-skinned, Catholic, Indian, poor, and Spanish-speaking—Mexicans and Mexican Americans have long suffered racial, religious, and cultural prejudices. Midwesterners have had much practice in despising Latinos, who come north to do the hardest and most poorly paid jobs, and who have been rejected, evicted, and even exiled. Resentment against Latinos has broadened and deepened over the last two decades as fears mount (especially in the Southwest and California) about a people whose population may soon surpass African Americans, whose language is believed to threaten the primacy of English, and whose masses are believed beyond assimilation.

For several decades Mexican and Mexican American migrants have worked in the sugar beet and, more recently, soybean fields of southern Minnesota. In a single short conversation with a few people in a convenience store along Highway 212, in a town where migrants are becoming year-long residents, we overheard the following remarks:

> "They don't work." "They are lazy." "They don't pay taxes. They work for cash." "They can live as we can't. So they can take those jobs." "Same as Indians." "They come up here to breed—incubate. They get pregnant down south and bring up a whole group of pregnant ones. Four times $750 equals a good living." "They come up early in March so they can start on their food stamps." "Can't keep 'em in school." "They drop out." "The youth are in your face with loud music." "Some come north to pick for vacation."

A list of distinctions was added by one of the participants in the conversation:

> "Don't trust those that have Minnesota plates. True migrants come from North Dakota, stop, and then continue on as far as Michigan." "Yes. Some are good workers, some are poor." "Some fit in and some don't." "They can do what we can't." "They work for rotten wages." "Yes, they may come from a terrible place, which makes this place seem okay."

Leaders should know that help and kindness will greet newcomers. So too will misunderstanding, confusion, and racism. Ranging from outright lies to half truths, prejudice and stereotypes will become common assumptions as newcomers threaten residents' sense of familiarity and order. Established residents may forget how hard and long Mexicans have worked the state's fields, and even how Hmong, Vietnamese, and Lao fought shoulder to shoulder with American forces in a losing war.

Housing and Geography

The meat-cutting industries make the new ethnic groups they bring to southwestern Minnesota into a new regional working class. Arriving without sufficient money or English language skills, the newcomers join the unskilled ranks of the meat- and poultry-processing industries. For them, there is only one place to work, one wage, and cheap housing. In this sense, the lives of these workers will be similar whether they are from Somalia or Ethiopia, Guatemala or Mexico, whether they live in Marshall, Worthington, or Madelia.

Assuming the average wage of these industries is $8 an hour, the newcomers' annual salary will be approximately $16,000 a year. To have this annual salary the workers must come and intend to stay. They must be able and willing to do physically taxing work for a year. At the same time, they must not get sick or seriously injured (no easy feat in an industry that averages a 27 percent injury rate for poultry, 42 percent for meat). Additionally, the company must offer workers at least fifty weeks of employment per year. If workers bring spouses who are able to work half time, their annual household incomes reach $24,000.

Their total income determines their housing, which, along with their work, determines their everyday lives. In turn, the cost of housing defines whether they can locate and establish themselves as residents in a given community. Home ownership is one of the key factors in whether newcomers will call a place home. A realistic calculation of the likelihood of newcomers buying homes in a community is made by measuring their estimated salary on the following "Housing Affordability Calculation."

TABLE 11

Housing Affordability Calculation

Annual Household Income	$ 15,000	$ 20,000	$ 30,000
Annual Household Non-Housing Expenditures			
Income Taxes	1,250	1,875	3,125
Food	3,177	3,742	4,219
Apparel and Services	790	1,080	1,465
Transportation	2,758	4,313	5,598
Health Care	1,484	1,666	1,579
Entertainment	726	943	1,292
Personal Care	256	286	349
Reading and Education	357	410	378
Miscellaneous	1,118	1,345	1,686
Personal Insurance and Pensions	678	1,116	1,986
Total Non-Housing Expenditures	$ 12,594	$ 16,776	$ 21,677
Annual Funds Remaining for Housing Expenditures	2,406	3,224	8,323
Monthly Funds Remaining for Housing Expenditures	200.50	268.67	693.58
Monthly Housing Non-Mortgage/Non-Rent Expense Allowance	246	268	314
Net Monthly Income Available for Mortgage Payment or Rent Payment	(46)	1	380
Affordable House Price	$ —	$ —	$ 47,227

Note: Housing affordability calculation was prepared utilizing Bureau of Labor Statistics Consumer Expenditure Survey Report February 1996 information.

Calculations of housing affordability do not consider that many ethnic newcomers send a considerable amount of their disposable income to their families living elsewhere. They do this as part of a strategy that accompanies and, in many cases, defines their migration. These calculations also omit crucial ethnic and cultural factors which—so important in defining the agricultural and community settlements of southwestern Minnesota—underpin a group's economic attitudes and activities.[1] Among these factors are a group's commitment to home ownership, its capacity for informal savings and loans within an extended family, and its willingness to undergo long-term abnegation for the sake of property ownership.

Availability of affordable housing itself and its proximity to the workplace determines where the newcomers live and how they spread out in the region. The simplest law is that they go where work is and seek affordable housing nearby. Although they tend to go where others of their kind are, they also choose to live where rents are cheapest. As they seek to rent and, later, own houses, they spread out into the nearby aging and declining towns which should have a surplus of larger and cheaper houses. In the case of a city like Marshall, where housing was both unavailable and unaffordable, the new work force first filled up the cheapest apartments, the few trailer courts, and then poured out into smaller neighboring communities like Tracy, Lynd, and other communities in Marshall's commuting area, making them working class suburbs.

The following chart identifies the available and affordable housing in the Marshall area.

[1]See Joseph A. Amato, *Servants of the Land: God, Family, and Farm, a Trinity of Belgian Economic Folkways in Southwestern Minnesota* (Marshall, Minn.: Crossings Press, 1990); John Radzilowski, *Out on the Wind: Poles and Danes in Lincoln County, Minnesota, 1880–1905* (Marshall, Minn.: Crossings Press, 1995).

TABLE 12

Median Housing Cost and Availability of Housing in Marshall Commuting Area

	Median House Value	Median Contract Rent	Homeowner Vacancy Rate (%)	Renter Vacancy Rate (%)
Marshall	$60,000	$279	1.2	8.2
Granite Falls	$45,600	$206	1.8	8.2
Cottonwood	$43,200	$179	2.0	9.2
Lynd	$35,000	$188	3.4	6.7
Minneota	$34,500	$178	2.5	13.6
Slayton	$34,200	$169	1.8	8.9
Ghent	$33,900	$192	2.1	NA
Canby	$27,600	$170	1.5	14.5
Tyler	$27,600	$209	2.6	10.2
Tracy	$27,500	$163	3.0	24.6
Lucan	$26,300	$150	1.3	21.4
Ivanhoe	$24,300	$131	2.5	10.0
Clarkfield	$24,200	$162	2.8	6.0
Milroy	$22,800	$158	NA	23.5
Balaton	$22,600	$178	0.9	NA
Lake Benton	$20,600	$125	1.9	11.3
Russell	$20,500	$180	1.4	23.3
Walnut Grove	$19,800	$119	2.4	16.7
Vesta	$18,800	$150	6.0	23.1
Hendricks	$18,700	$133	4.0	13.9
Taunton	$18,100	$180	3.2	8.3
Hanley Falls	$17,500	$150	4.4	16.7
St. Leo	$17,100	$150	2.2	33.3
Porter	$15,000	$113	NA	28.6
Hazel Run	$15,000	$113	NA	NA
Florence	$15,000	$100	8.3	33.3
Garvin	$15,000	$150	3.4	15.4
Echo	$15,000	$169	2.7	9.7
Wood Lake	$15,000	$146	2.8	2.9

Source: 1990 Bureau of the Census

It is too soon to describe patterns of new workers and the emerging ethnic settlements throughout southwestern Minnesota. The case of the large Lao community in Mountain Lake shows that newcomers may work in one place and build their community elsewhere. On the other hand, members of the resident community may flee from and seek to segregate the newcomers. They may do this through zoning ordinances, especially regarding the location of trailer courts, fixing prices of sales and rentals, and the transfer of their children to alternative schools under the open-enrollment act.

In any case, a new southwestern Minnesota is being born out of the decline of traditional agricultural villages, towns, and cities; the emergence of new industries and the appearance of new workers; and the formation of new ethnic communities and corridors. The cultural and social geography of southwestern Minnesota is being dramatically transformed. Preliminary portraits of the following nine communities—Marshall, Tracy, Lynd, Worthington, St. James, Mountain Lake, Madelia, Montevideo, and Willmar—offer a view of a region in the making.

Marshall

Marshall is an emerging regional center and county seat. With a population of 12,000, it has more than half of Lyon County's population. It escaped the prevalent regional population decline in the 1980s. It has many small businesses, a handful of large industries—Schwan's Sales Enterprises (a major food processor), Minnesota Corn Processors (which makes ethanol, corn syrup, and starch), Heartland Food Company (which processes turkeys), and two electronics firms, Schott Corporation and B & H Electronics, as well as a four-year university, Southwest State University. In 1995 it was ranked high in the book *The 100 Best Small Towns in America.*

As a regional and university center, newcomers and minorities are not new to Marshall. In the early part of this century the town was home to a large French-Canadian minority which moved elsewhere in the years between the World Wars. Icelanders, French Canadians, Czechs, Poles, and even a small number of Mexicans have migrated in and out, depending on labor markets and conditions on the farms. Belgians migrated in and stayed. Marshall did not entirely escape farm protest in the 1930s and 1950s, and war protest and student activism from its new college in the early 1970s. Since its founding, minorities have come and gone from the college. Black students did not find Marshall hospitable in the early 1970s, a period when the nation had its sharpest elbows out. Iranian students came in considerable numbers to the university for a few years in the 1970s, only to leave in the aftermath of America's conflict with their homeland. In the late 1970s and early 1980s, Vietnamese refugee families came to Marshall with the help of the Lutheran Church and stayed (as they did elsewhere in southwestern Minnesota) a few years before seeking homes in California or in the Twin Cities, where large, rooted communities exist.

Marshall's most recent experience with minorities came with the arrival of Heartland Foods. A branch of Willmar Poultry Company, Heartland Food Co. took over the Swift-Eckrich plant in 1988 and continued employing about half of its 358 workers. Spurred on by its Chamber of Commerce and the Marshall Industries Foundation, and afraid to lose one of its major employers—particularly amidst a climate defined by the farm crisis and talk of rural decline—the city council, county board, and school board granted Heartland $500,000 in Tax Increment Financing (an arrangement where taxes are turned into bonds which finance plant and industry development). The following year the city officials endorsed Heartland's $2.7 million application for a low-interest loan from the Minnesota Economic and Development Board for the purchase of the plant.

Hearings on these matters did not consider what sort of neighbor a new packing plant would make. Nor were more precise questions raised about who would fill the unskilled jobs at Heartland, where they would live, and how they would be treated. In 1994–95, the plant processed 170,369,840 pounds of turkey. It paid a $6-an-hour starting wage, with bonuses for attendance, group health, and additional wages for the night shift. Its public description of its work force over the last five years shows a steady but not severe decline in the number of non-minority workers (who make up the great bulk of the managers); a quick rise then steady decline in Asian workers (some of whom have gone to work in one of the city's two electronics firms); a sudden arrival of Somalis followed by a precipitous decline in their numbers; and, consistent with the industry as a whole, a shift towards the Hispanicization of the labor force. Employment figures from the town's two electronics firms show that, aside from some Africans at Schott Corp., few minorities have gone to work for these firms, each of which employs just over 100 people.

Above all other companies, Heartland has meant tumult in Marshall from its beginning. It had a first-year worker turnover rate of 255 percent. In the first year, it had single-day turnover rates higher than 15 percent. With so many new, transitory, and foreign employees, who in vast majority were single males, Heartland created a sense of great change in a quiet, and what by most accounts was an overpoliced city.

Negative events overshadowed positive developments. There were individual incidents, including a bomb threat at Heartland in 1991 and a stabbing in the plant in 1994. In December 1995, a couple was found living in their car. They had come all the way from Las Cruces, New Mexico, to Marshall to discover that Heartland was not hiring at the time. (There was an outpouring of sympathy for the couple, who found work in Worthington.)

Other negative incidents involved the company's entire work force. The Immigration and Naturalization Service raided the plant in May 1993. The raid cost the company 100 employees, 81 of whom were illegal, and left 450,000 turkeys unprocessed. Heartland responded by recruiting more than 70 people from Eagle Pass and El Paso, Texas. Almost 40 percent of those from Eagle Pass left in four months, complaining about low wages, poor treatment, and safety concerns. One of the workers Heartland let go claimed he was dismissed for advocating workers' interests. A subsequent INS raid on Heartland netted another large group of undocumented workers.

Another bitter labor incident occurred in 1993. At one crack Heartland dismissed 82 of its 150 Somali workers, who formed approximately 25 percent of its entire work force. The Somalis had recently come as a group to work at Heartland in the wake of the closing of the Sioux Falls John Morrell plant. When 13 Somalis were fired over a contested work break, 69 others protested in sympathy by either walking off the job or not showing up the next day. They, in turn, were fired. The company union's protest was useless. The paper was bannered by headlines of Somali workers charging racism and company complaints about bad Somali work habits and its justifications about the need for industrial discipline.

Outside the plant, newcomers were identified with crime. Somalis allegedly drove far too casually for local drivers. At the courthouse, unmarried Somali women appeared for benefits with their "male friends" or "drivers." A group of Hmong was arrested after stealing weapons from the local sports store. Hispanic dances frequently ended in serious fights, one of which, in December 1995, resulted in three injured police officers. In July 1995, with the help of the Mexican consulate, one Mexican worker charged that he was not paid, and in addition he was shackled, threatened with a gun, and involuntarily held on a nearby farmstead by another Hispanic newcomer against whom similar charges had been leveled in the past. In a battle to control workers' loyalties, one group of Mexicans severely beat a member of a rival group with a chain. Two recent murders in the Marshall vicinity—one in 1993 and another in 1994—had Hispanic perpetrators. Both crimes, one particularly cruel and involving a Hispanic Heartland employee, drew considerable attention because murders are rare in southwestern Minnesota and they required prolonged searches for their perpetrators.

A local judge described the overall climate of the first years of Heartland's expansion as "rough." Many of its employees who came before his bench were, in his words, "only one step ahead of the law." Concern, fear, and prejudice escalated with the rising crime rates.

Housing issues proved among the most complex for Heartland and the most painful for its new employees. They added to the sense of disorder and turbulence surrounding the industry and its new employees. In November 1990, in order to provide housing for ten, and possibly twenty-five to thirty-five more Lao and Hmong families, Heartland began to negotiate for housing with the surrounding communities of Lynd and Tracy. The company even purchased some condemned houses in Marshall and moved them to Lynd for the new families, who eventually left. Heartland bought trailers in Tracy's trailer court, "Frog Alley," which it rented to its workers. (A January 1993 fire tragically killed two daughters of a Heartland employee who later successfully contended that Heartland was negligent for failing to provide a fire extinguisher for the trailer.) Facing a severe shortage of available inexpensive housing to rent or buy, in the summer of 1992 Heartland rented dorm rooms at Southwest State University for 100 of its employees.

While the housing shortage caused problems, it saved the city from much of the turbulence that can come with days of expansion. Many of Heartland's newcomers worked in Marshall but lived elsewhere. With vacant houses and declining numbers, Tracy and Lynd welcomed those who overflowed Marshall's trailer courts, available apartments, occasional run-down houses, and its Main Street Marshall Hotel (whose owner was fined for unsafe housing conditions). Marshall's recent decision to build 50 units of low-cost housing provoked strong resistance which one city leader described as racist. Ironically, even this housing may be too costly for most $6- to $7-an-hour workers in a city where the most economical homes range between $60,000 and $80,000.

Limited by housing shortages and Heartland's stagnant demand for labor, a calm has returned to Marshall. City and county institutions appear able to handle their new loads. According to the director of Region VIII North social services, at the end of 1995 minority newcomers, after their first six months, do not use social services any more than anyone else. They are here to work. In Lyon County, there are 41 Asian cases, involving 175 persons; 100 Hispanic cases, involving 361 persons; and 8 Somali cases, with 19 persons. Collectively, they form part of a total caseload of 2,511, which involves 5,497 people. When combined with a handful of American Indians, Puerto-Ricans, and African Americans, minorities constitute a total caseload of 176, involving 805 clients, which equals 6.9 percent of total cases and 14.6 percent of total clients.

Marshall police report a decline in crime. In 1995, *The 100 Best Small Towns in America* ranked Marshall 24th in the crime category, with 2,397 crimes compared to the national average of 5,928. In January 1996, the chief of police reported that crime is: "Not a problem. Things are improving." The March 8, 1996, issue of the Marshall *Independent* led off with the headline

"Marshall Crime Report Filled With Low Figures," and reported that the "city of Marshall experienced no homicides, aggravated rapes, robberies, acts of arson, or motor vehicle-related deaths in 1995." In comparison to four other communities of its size in the state, it had the fewest auto thefts, criminal sexual conduct incidents, arson cases, burglaries, and robberies. Serious crimes in the city, which ranged from murder and assault to manslaughter and auto theft, had declined since 1991, and the "Hispanic" proportion of them appeared in 1994 to have started to taper off. In 1991, of 194 serious crimes, 16 were reportedly committed by Hispanics; of 157 in 1992, 23 were perpetrated by Hispanics; of 173 in 1993, 49 were committed by Hispanics; and in 1994, 38 of 160 were reported with Hispanic perpetrators. (County arrest records, which distinguished some minorities, sex, and adults and juveniles, did not distinguish ethnic and cultural groups.)

Marshall schools report a stable and nonviolent atmosphere. Superintendent Gerald Huber reported the following information: In late fall of 1995, there were 208 minorities with 95 Hispanics (the largest group), followed by 56 Asians, and 55 blacks and others. In conformity with more families and fewer single males, the number of government-defined minorities in the schools went up from 155 (66 of whom were Hispanic) in 1993–94 to 200 in 1994–95 (composed of 70 Asians and 75 Hispanics). Suggesting the general movement of newcomers to the region, the total transfers into the high school were 92, 27 of whom were minorities; of the 102 transfers out of the high school (including dropouts), 23 were minorities. (The Hispanics accounted for all 8 dropouts.) Hispanics are coming in from Mexico, Texas, other locations in rural Minnesota, and the Twin Cities area, while those transferring out are going to other states and elsewhere in rural Minnesota. The superintendent's primary concern is the absence of participation by minority children in extracurricular activities, a concern school officials have traditionally had about immigrant and ethnic communities.

Tracy

By housing Marshall's working-class newcomers, Tracy experiences directly much of what Marshall causes. At least this has been the case during the past five years.

Once a regional center and a county competitor with Marshall, Tracy has gone the way of the big railroad yard that made the town and defined its pride, and still resonates in its annual celebration, "Tracy Box Car Days." In the 1980s, rural decline came to stay in Tracy. Like the rest of rural Minnesota, Tracy was experiencing an aging and declining population, a lagging business and real estate market, and no salvation in sight.

All this made Tracy willing to take chances. Starting in the early 1990s, Tracy opened its door to Heartland's new Hispanic and Hmong workers. It shared the hope, suffered the tumult, felt the pain, and has begun to reap some of the benefits of the risk.

Methodist minister, Rev. Wesly Gable, likens his experience working with newcomers to being an overseas missionary. He has seen Hmong form their own church with 60 children and 15 core families. They hold services at Tracy Lutheran Church. This marks both a failure to have them join his congregation (something for which he and his church had worked aggressively), and a triumph of independence for the town's small community of Hmong.

He found it more difficult to make contact with "the transient" Latinos. The church welcomed Heartland's decision to take over the trailer court. Members did what they could to be hospitable and to proselytize. They showed up with food, and seeing the destitute conditions in which the people lived, they returned with bedding, blankets, and basic goods. The first Hispanics who came in the fall of 1992 lasted no more than six months—cold and lack of work played a part in their return south.

It was, Rev. Gable suggested, as if the church was ministering to a whirlwind. The Methodist congregation took in a family of six that was living in a car. They brought fifty new minority members into their church community, and one month later not a single one of them was still in attendance. "They offered us a taste of what it was like to be a missionary church."

The dialogue Tracy started with Heartland in November 1992 became constant and had positive results after the January 1993 fire in Tracy's "Frog Alley" trailer park killed two small children. Yet 1993 proved to be the most tumultuous year of all. Ten percent of Tracy's population—220 people—used the food shelf in July 1993.

The town's Hispanics, who came in considerable numbers in 1993, did not prove to be a cohesive group, which added to the confusion on all sides. These newcomers were documented and undocumented; uneducated and college-educated; and speakers of English, Spanish, and Indian languages. The newcomers came from all along the Texas border, throughout Mexico, as well as Guatemala, Cuba, and other areas of Latin America. Many were single males, 18 to 24, some of whom drank and committed crimes. Domestic disputes were common.

Tracy experienced its first murder in 90 years in July 1993. Heartland employee Ramon Guardiola, a father of four, was found dead in a culvert. He was a likable, well-known, hardworking, fifty-two-year-old former truck driver from Eagle Pass, Texas. According to a newspaper account, he loved to hunt and fish and was in Tracy to find a better life for his family. He was bludgeoned and then drowned in a ditch by three young Mexican American men, former Heartland employees. Their motive was robbery. A murder the following year in a Tracy home by a Hispanic and his girlfriend, their capture, and trials that followed in 1995 suggested the price the city paid for its welcome to newcomers. Tracy residents began to lock their doors.

The mayor of Tracy, John Almlie, has been at the center of the city's experience with the newcomers. He encouraged them to come to Tracy. He helped seek a revolving low-interest housing loan fund for them. He argued that their presence benefitted the town's businesses and schools. He attended a Hmong picnic of two hundred, to which relatives, clan members, and friends came from St. Paul. Despite the real cultural differences, he felt a special bond was forming between them. At the same time, he stood with the Hispanics when prejudice swelled against them in the wake of the two murders. He cannot forget how, down in the grave, he accepted the coffins of the two dead children burned in the Frog Alley fire, and later stood next to the parents as they threw the first shovelsful of dirt down onto their children's caskets.

Tracy has invested a part of itself in these newcomers, and it has not gone entirely unrewarded. As the number of undocumented and single males diminishes, families stay and start to take root. Most Hmong and Laotians have their own homes. Social worker Jan Otto reports that some minority women are presently serving as nurses' aides. The newcomers' children are dedicated to school (especially the Hmong and Laotians) and learning English. (There are sufficient Spanish-speaking teachers and a Spanish language course so many of the Hispanic children can learn their native tongue.) A number of the students, according to Tracy school superintendent Harold Remme, are becoming more involved in extracurricular activities, although cultural traditions and fear of injury have limited sports activity.

Things still remain to be done. Language proves one of the most profound obstacles blocking newcomers. It stands between parents and children, patients and doctors, newcomers and host institutions. In the case of Tracy, goodwill and tragedy are the crucibles out of which a new community is being born.

Lynd

Lynd is another important residence for Heartland's new minority workers. Lynd, a small town of 350, only five miles to the southwest of Marshall, once the county seat of Lyon County—with only a bar, grocery store, ball diamond, and school—is now a mere bedroom community.

Perched on the side of a hill, defined by the descending Redwood River, and standing at the eastern entrance to Camden State Park, Lynd has an attractiveness few of the region's towns have. However, it attracts poor and minority workers not because of its desirable setting but because it provides cheap and convenient housing.

With a large trailer court, which holds approximately 25 vehicles, and only a handful of houses worth more than $60,000 (median house value was $35,000 in 1990), Lynd afforded the cheap housing and real estate that Marshall did not. In its first year, Heartland even purchased and moved eight houses into the north end of Lynd along the river, with plans to rent and eventually sell them to the families of its new Hmong employees.

Of course, especially in the first years, minorities (particularly Hispanics) brought new problems and challenges to Lynd. Yet, at the same time, the children of minorities have helped satisfy Lynd's oldest and strongest dream: to keep its grade school open. (Until a decade ago, Lynd's longest and most passionate battles involved keeping its high school open.)

However, minorities have not added to Lynd's sense of stability. In the spring of 1996, only one student—from a non–

English-speaking Mexican family—has been at the Lynd school for as long as three years. The Hmong children and their families, in whom the town and school had invested so much energy, goodwill, and hope, are all gone, except for one original family of renters. Somehow the Hmong never got hold of the houses they were promised, and they left. The company houses are now rented by Hispanic employees of Heartland. Some eighty other minority newcomers live in the trailer court.

There is a certain tone of disappointment on the part of Lynd's teachers and leaders. The town's new people seem as impermanent as the waters of Redwood River which, arising out of the great western Buffalo Ridge, flow east—down through Lynd to Marshall—to the Minnesota and the Mississippi rivers.

Worthington

Worthington stands in sharp contrast to Marshall. Indeed, it is precisely because of the similarity between the size of the two cities and their function as county seats and regional centers that differences between them are so pronounced.

Comparable statistics for the two towns show that Worthington is poorer, older, smaller, less dynamic, and supported by a narrower job base. Its service area is smaller as well. Wages tend to be lower in Worthington, and the average value of housing is lower as well. Unlike Marshall, Worthington had an excess of housing that Marshall did not. Rents in Worthington were an average of $20 a month cheaper.

In contrast to Marshall, Worthington is more turbulent and less settled. Worthington seems astir, off guard, perplexed, and uncertain of its direction. A portion of its resident population is fearful of newcomers and the changes they have brought. This sense of disorder and unsettledness seems to have nothing to do with lack of goodwill on the part of its civil leaders. In fact, Worthington responded quickly to the large influx of immigrants by forming, in 1991, the "Cultural Diversity Coalition." At its peak, the group had as many as 100 people involved in ten different work groups addressing a wide range of issues from housing to translators as well as racism and law enforcement. Working in conjunction with the University of Minnesota Extension Service, the city expanded its traditional 4-H program to include a Latino 4-H club. (The University of Minnesota Extension Service has also funded the Community Connectors in Nobles, Lyon, Watonwan, Brown and Cottonwood counties. Community Connectors are hired to serve as a link between immigrant groups and the resources and agencies of the larger community.)

Worthington's condition seems primarily a condition of the sheer number of newcomers who appeared in such a short period of time. The turbulence is suggested not only by the mounting numbers of new and strange neighbors, but the steady increase of crime since 1989 when the newcomers began to arrive. Between 1989 and 1994, according to its police chief, complaints have increased almost 60 percent, juvenile crime 48 percent, and adult crime a staggering 195 percent. Worthington, which has never experienced a single murder, has seen arrests for assault double since 1989. Gang activity is increasing, as is drug dealing. The city has experienced eight drive-by shootings in the last five years, two in 1995.

Worthington's turbulence is a function of its past. Worthington stopped growing by 1970, and there it remained until the late 1980s. At that time Worthington was in a period of gentle decline, characterized by a shrinking and aging population and a weakening business community.

Worthington's population numbers confirm this view. After the most modest growth of approximately 1 percent a year across the 1950s and 1960s, Worthington reached 10,000 inhabitants. With only a slight dip in the 1980 census, it remained there until 1990. The population of surrounding Nobles County declined 8 percent in the 1980s, partly a function of a 14 percent out-migration during the decade. In contrast, Marshall, from 1950 to 1970, had gone from 6,000 to 10,000 inhabitants and, between 1970 and 1990, from 10,000 to 12,000. Its county lost less than 2 percent, and its out-migration approached 9 percent.

Worthington held its own in the 1990 census because of an influx of newcomers. Its minority population accounted for 634 of its residents in 1990, almost 2,000 in 1995, and, it is predicted, 2,250 or more in 2000. Marshall's minority population went from approximately 300 in 1990, to 1,000 in 1995, to, it is predicted, only 800 in 2000. In 2000 Worthington's minorities may account for almost 25 percent of the city's population, while they will constitute only approximately 6 percent of

Marshall's inhabitants. (Unlike Worthington, Marshall has not gone out of its way to provide housing for the newcomers.)

Ethnic diversity characterizes Worthington's new minorities. Its Hispanics are primarily from the Texas border and from Mexico, but they also come from California, Guatemala, Honduras, Puerto Rico, and Cuba. Its Asians—to show how simplifying if not distorting government categories are—not only include a handful of earlier Vietnamese, new Cambodians, and Thai, but also Lao and Hmong, who identified themselves as belonging to at least five groups. Its Africans also defy simple classification. They include peoples from Somalia, Sudan, Kenya, and Ethiopia, whose commitment to traditional dress made them vulnerable to winter winds that literally blew many out of town. The police, who wished to discuss an ill-clad child with an Ethiopian father, had to use AT&T's language-line before locating in San Francisco a person who spoke the near-extinct language, Ankah.

One industry accounts for this rich diversity. Swift & Company, an independent operating company of ConAgra, Inc., has defined Worthington's dramatic transformation and its growth. Swift & Company more than doubled its work force in the last five years, which went from approximately 750 to 1,500. Its annual turnover rate averages 80 percent.

Outside writers are tempted to make the essence of Worthington a comparison and contrast of its two main industries: Swift & Company, the pork processor, and Campbell Soup, the local food processor. They ignore a public school system of 500 employees; a small community college of 600 students, founded in the 1930s; Bedford, a maker of plastic goods which employs 400; and Highland, a trailer and mobile home manufacturer which hires 200 workers. As if one is writing a morality play, Campbell's has a reputation for being fair and seeking to accommodate its workers. With a work force of about 600, the approximate size of Marshall's Heartland Foods, its turnover rate is 4 percent a year. Last year it experienced a 5 percent turnover rate, which the company judged to be unsatisfactory. (The community welcomed its recent $18 million plant investment.) Conversely, Swift & Company makes

Worthington a turnstile for the coming and going of a large population. On the basis of turnover rates alone, it could be argued that Swift & Company—which pays approximately the same wage as Campbell's—is sixteen times less attractive to workers than Campbell's. Even though this comparison may overlook other factors, it opens the door for speculation about the difference between the two industries in general and benefits and amenities offered by the two companies in particular.

As of April 1, 1990, Swift & Company had 756 workers, while it had 1,468 workers in 1994, and 1,569 in 1995. Minorities (with varying male-female ratios from 2:1 to 4:1) fill the ranks of unskilled workers. Consistent with the industry as a whole as enumerated in Table 13, Swift & Company's numbers for the last four years suggest a constant core of Caucasian employees, many of whom are managers, on the one hand, and a Hispanicization of the overall work force on the other.

TABLE 13

**Ethnicity of Swift & Company Employees–
Worthington (Minnesota) Plant**

	Jan. 31, 1991		Jan. 31, 1995		Jan. 31, 1996	
Caucasian	669	71.9%	698	44.1%	687	42.9%
Hispanic	119	12.8%	442	28.0%	525	32.8%
Asian	126	13.5%	337	21.3%	324	20.3%
Black	16	1.7%	104	6.6%	64	4.0%
Total	930	100.0%	1,581	100.0%	1,600	100.0%

Source: Swift & Company

Given the low turnover rate at Campbell's and the seemingly low diffusion rate of newcomers into the city's overall labor force, Swift & Company's turnover rate translates directly into the city's entrance and exit rate. Worthington Mayor Robert J. Demuth insists there are less than 5 percent minority workers in any company or institution in town outside of

Swift & Company and Campbell's. Police Chief Don Linssen indirectly confirms this by suggesting that those who know English well find a lot of work translating. Swift & Company's annual turnover rate of 80 percent accounted for the entrance and exit of 2,510 workers in 1995 when it had a work force of 1,569. If each worker belonged to a household size of three, Swift & Company would have accounted for bringing 3,765 newcomers into Worthington that year. Although this estimate is far too high, in any given year, Swift & Company's high turnover rate might account for approximately 2,000 newcomers.

A consequence of the static and aging quality of Worthington's population in the 1970s and 1980s, available housing has meant that the workers who came to work in Worthington also lived there. Only recently have newcomers begun to spread out into the countryside for affordable housing.

The consequence of worker turnover is also experienced in the city's schools. The new minorities who fill the school transfer in and out in large numbers. Many newcomers need training in English as well as in their own language to prepare them to study English. One grade school principal reported that without minority enrollment he would have to lay off 25 percent of his teachers. Despite the rising numbers of minority newcomers, the school system predicts a long-term overall decline in future numbers. Their projections are based on an aging host population and the assumption of continuing high turnover in the minority community, which is characterized by an unmarried and highly mobile labor force.

The experience of one Worthington grade school confirms the importance of minority youths to the school system and the sense of change they bring to it. Caucasians make up 74 percent of the school, Hispanics 14 percent, Asians and others 12 percent. Of the 86 Hispanic students, almost one-third of those enrolled at the beginning of the 1995–96 school year have left, while two-thirds (63 percent) of all Hispanic children are new arrivals in the district this year.

Other factors also have been disturbing. A combination of

increased police visits to the school, the tendency of some minority youths to take the law into their own hands, and the appearance of outside groups of youths entering the schools led Worthington to initiate a safe-school campaign this year. Mutual understanding between established residents and newcomers is still only a hope in the schools.

Compounding the problem of prejudice are the clear class differences between groups—particularly between Caucasians and Hispanics. At one Worthington grade school, 94 percent of Hispanic children receive free or reduced-cost lunches; among Laotian children, 65 percent receive this assistance; only 25 percent of Caucasian children get free or reduced lunches. Similarly, most newcomer students require some English as a Second Language (ESL) training. Nearly 85 percent of all minority students come from non-English-speaking households.

Disturbances in the city's school fed a traditional regional resentment against Worthington as the dominant lead city. In the opinion of one school official, this animus and traditional stereotype and prejudice might account for a significant part of the sixty students who transferred out of Worthington under Open Enrollment to nearby towns, Rushmore and Adrian. These transfers deserve examination as well as do the subjects of zoning and resident flight aimed at evading minority newcomers. (A fifth-grade class in nearby Adrian, in the spring of 1995, described the current immigrants in "our area" as doing the following things: starting gangs, engaging in drive-by shootings, taking jobs from Americans, killing each other, robbing people, spreading diseases, harassing people, vandalizing, making the town look bad, bringing health risks, crowding the country, bringing and selling drugs, kidnapping, making bomb threats, raping, swearing, stealing, blackmailing, and bringing weapons to school.)

Quoted in a *Wall Street Journal* article (Oct. 31, 1995), Jerry Fiola—leader of Worthington's Cultural Diversity Coalition—spoke for many when he said, "The town that people who have lived here all their lives remember is gone. It no longer exists." Fiola went on to say, "The newcomers didn't just stumble into Worthington. They were lured here by ConAgra, Inc., which in 1989 decided to expand its pork-processing plant and hire an additional 400 workers." Faced by near full employment and "local people unwilling to cut and debone hogs for $7.50 an hour, ConAgra attracted workers from Mexico as well as immigrants from Vietnam, Laos, and Africa."

On the issue of change, Mayor Demuth distinguishes three distinct groups of Worthington's citizens. There are the old who don't acknowledge the change in their town. Then there are those who perceive the change but don't care. Finally, there are those who accept the change and are enthused about its promise. In his opinion, the latter account for what successes Worthington has had in the past five years, which includes hosting an annual international festival in July. The festival features soccer teams from Minnesota and nearby states as well as art and food booths, and it draws thousands of people.

Worthington has had other successes as well. For the short term it has staved off decline. Many of the city's institutions have been revived. For example, the Bigelow Christian Reformed Church, once on the verge of closing, now has 100 families—90 percent Laotian or Vietnamese. A handful of stores—an Asian food store, a Mexican and a Thai restaurant, a Vietnamese billiards parlor, and a Spanish-language video shop—add to the town's diversity. Some minorities, especially those who know English, have found jobs at other companies. Campbell's, a preferred work site, has a 35 to 40 percent minority employment rate. Home ownership, especially among Asians, is on the rise. The mayor estimates 90 to 100 minority families are homeowners. In a word, a core of newcomers has begun to call Worthington home.

But it seems that the leaders are still not confident about what they have wrought. No one yet has a way to calculate the economic and social costs of such things as additional translators and law enforcement officers versus the benefits of school revenue and added economic activity. No one can offer them a means to weigh gains from escaping a decline in population versus costs of increased numbers of an underpaid and largely migrant working class. Furthermore, Worthington's leaders lack the means to weigh loss of security, order, and familiarity. So they go ahead issue by issue, lacking an overall plan. They know they are carrying on an experiment in which they do not control the variables nor share a common goal.

The uncertainty of Worthington's leaders may be attributed to many causes. They have no sure understanding of what it means to live in a time of turbulence equalled only by the region's first years of settlement. They are being asked to understand how Worthington's present transformation belongs to world and national immigration and economic patterns. More precisely, they have yet to confront the turnover rate of a single company that leaves the town spinning and casts doubt on the kind of home Worthington will be for anyone in the future. All serious dialogue over the city's future—its immigrants, their number, and success or failure at absorption—must start by focusing on that turnover rate, its implications, and how it can be curtailed.

St. James and Mountain Lake

Not all towns have the same ethnic groups and the same experiences with the minority newcomers. Two regional cities, both with a high percentage of newcomers but differing experiences, are St. James and Mountain Lake.

With a population of 4,452, St. James has defied the general trend for Watonwan County. From 1980 to 1990, Watonwan County lost 5.49 percent of its population, but in the same period the population of St. James remained nearly constant. In the five years since, St. James has grown even more rapidly than in the previous ten years, and 20 percent of its population is Hispanic. At one time as much as 20 percent of the Hispanic population was composed of illegal aliens. Although there are other newcomers in St. James, their numbers are insignificant.

With a population of 1,906, Mountain Lake is a little less than half the size of St. James. Nevertheless, its numbers too have grown, thanks to an influx of newcomers. Laotians make up the largest group, with 45 to 50 Laotian families (120 to 140 individuals) residing in Mountain Lake. As in the case of St. James, there are other newcomers in Mountain Lake, but not in significant numbers for this study.

St. James has two major employers of newcomers—Tony Downs Foods and Swift-Eckrich. Both are food-processing plants. In the late 1980s, Tony Downs hired representatives in the Rio Grande Valley in Texas to recruit as many workers as possible for their processing plant. Buses were sent to Texas to pick up the new employees, who were hired for three-month stints.

When Swift-Eckrich took over the former Monfort plant, many more Hispanics came to town. By a "gentlemen's agreement," Swift-Eckrich will not actively recruit employees from Tony Downs, but many who start out at Tony Downs end up at Swift-Eckrich because the pay is better.

In contrast to St. James, Mountain Lake has no large employer of minorities, but it has available housing. For most of its minority workers, Mountain Lake is a bedroom community supplying housing for workers from Swift-Eckrich and Tony Downs in St. James, Caldwell Packing and Toro in Windom, and a food-processing plant in Butterfield. In contrast to the Hispanic employees from St. James, there is little employee turnover among Mountain Lake's Laotian workers.

About 25 percent of the children enrolled in the St. James school system are Hispanic. Many of them speak Spanish but cannot read or write it. Consequently, the school district hires special teachers to help these students learn Spanish, and to be interpreters for Spanish-speaking parents. Although this is an added expense, it is important to note that the children of newcomers bring $1 million of state aid into St. James' schools.

Data on St. James' schools reveal much about its Hispanic newcomers and how they are redefining school, city, and region. Of 1,311 students in the school system in 1994–95, 192 or about 15.5 percent (about equally male and female) were classified as Hispanic. There were only 16, or a little more than 1 percent, classified as Asians. In 1995–96, school enrollment had increased to 1,376, primarily as a result of a corresponding increase of Hispanics to 239 or 17.3 percent. Asians declined to 13 students.

Aside from numbers, Hispanic students affect the school in other ways. About 60 percent of the Hispanics are enrolled in English as a Second Language (ESL) classes. These numbers are doubled in grades K–3. Hispanic students are relatively evenly distributed across K–9, with a slight drop in the number of males thereafter. Most immigrant children do not participate in the range of school activities. Apart from four in advanced art, none are in advanced classes such as math, chemistry, or physics. A significant handful do participate in sports: Last fall and winter, seven participated in football, one in tennis, one in cross-country, and six in wrestling.

In 1994–95, of the total 58 transfers into grades 7–12, 36 were Hispanic; with an additional 8 readmittances of the 65 students who left the district, 27 being Hispanics. Of the 58 who transferred into the school, 12 came from other Minnesota schools, 19 from another state, 4 from another country. More revealing, of the 33 students who transferred into grades 4–6, 9 came from an adjacent county, 5 from elsewhere in outstate Minnesota, 2 from other states, 13 from Texas, and 4 from Mexico. Of the 33 who transferred out, 6 transferred to elsewhere in rural Minnesota, 10 to Texas, and 7 to other states. In grades K–3, of the 61 who transferred in, 9 came from within the county or from an adjacent county, 15 from Texas, 4 from another state, and 7 from Mexico. Of the 33 who transferred out, 3 stayed in the county or an adjacent county, 3 went elsewhere in rural Minnesota, 10 went to Texas, and 7 to another state.

This information suggests that Hispanic newcomers to St. James are coming from largely Spanish-speaking cultures on one side of the border or the other. (Many families arrive without a single member of the family speaking English.) By far the greatest number of newcomers are connected to Texas. For a significant number, Texas is their point of entry into the United States and a short-term staging point for migration north. For a yet larger number, Texas belongs to a long-established migration chain that links the U.S.-Mexico border to the rural Midwest and southern Minnesota. This notion squares with Superintendent Kent Nelson's observation, "There is generally an influx of transfers from Texas/Mexico in mid to late fall, and while there are many ins and outs during the year, there is a noticeable increase in numbers of students transferring back in May." At the same time, the data offered here suggests that those who are coming directly from Mexico are not returning to Mexico or Texas but going on to other rural locations in Minnesota and other states. St. James is the starting point in the U.S. immigration.

St. James received a grant to address the problem of work

interference with parent-school relations and communications. Tony Downs and Swift-Eckrich will allow a liaison from the school to meet with parents during lunch break. Participants hope that the businesses, schools, parents, and children will all benefit from improved communications.

In recent months, progressive St. James leaders—a mixture of school officials, lawyers, and political leaders—have begun to work on two very difficult issues. In conjunction with the Blandin Foundation, they are seeking ways to enter into contact with the town's new minorities who lack identifiable leaders. Recognizing that literacy is a primary condition of newcomers' acceptance into the community, they received a two-year, $200,000 grant, in conjunction with Madelia, to identify literacy levels of its immigrants and offer a Spanish General Education Degree.

Of a total of 590 students in grades K–12 in the Mountain Lake Public School system, 101 are Southeast Asian, 30 are Hispanic, and 4 are black. Thus, newcomers make up 22 percent of the students in the Mountain Lake school system. In the words of a Mountain Lake school official, "There is no doubt that without the minorities Mountain Lake would have had to merge or combine its school district by now." The first Laotians to reach Mountain Lake were well educated, most having served as government workers or in some other leadership capacity. Then Laotians of peasant backgrounds came. Many of their children came from refugee camps where education is an unattainable luxury. Nevertheless, education is important to the Laotian people, and in 1995 there were seven Laotian students in the Mountain Lake graduating class. Three were among the 12 honor students. If a Laotian child is absent, the school routinely sends a "runner" out to check on the student because the family has no phone. The Mountain Lake school district offers day-care in the school, and some Laotian families bring their children. Many Laotian families came to the small community of Mountain Lake to escape gangs in the larger cities.

Mountain Lake has an excellent eighth-grade basketball team made up of Laotian players. According to Jim Brandt, an

ESL instructor, to a great extent participation in sports depends on whether or not the group leader is involved in them. In Mountain Lake, starting in about eighth grade, there has been an increased interest in extracurricular participation by minorities.

Hispanics in St. James attend church services in one of several denominations. They also have their own churches where Spanish is the language of the service. Several Hispanics attend services at St. James Catholic Church but, according to Fr. Richard Riordan, it is difficult to pinpoint the exact number who belong to the parish because they are extremely mobile. In the last five years St. James has seen an increase in Hispanic baptisms; there were 26 in 1995. Most of the baptisms are of children, some up to three years old. Fr. Riordan has performed "a few" Hispanic marriages, but not interracial marriages, although there have been "a couple" of interracial births. Most churches can be counted on in emergencies: providing money for gas, food, rent, medicine, and electricity. The churches want the new minorities to know they care. It is interesting that the new minorities turn to the churches quite often, but when they do, they want to "talk to Father."

Laotians have started their own Christian congregation in Mountain Lake. Their leader is Pastor Tong Chitchalerntham. He is a leader for the Laotian population and serves as a liaison with the host community. Since the Laotians tend to be more stable than the Hispanics, Pastor Tong knows his congregation well, as almost all of the Laotian community attend his temple.

Law enforcement officials in St. James and in Mountain Lake both report increased crime since the influx of newcomers to their towns. In St. James the crime rate has doubled since the Hispanics became a large part of the population. At least 50 percent of all arrest warrants are for Hispanics. According to law enforcement officials in Mountain Lake, their crime rate has also risen since new minorities arrived in town. As with the rest of society, it is young, adult males who are most often involved in crime. A high rate of recidivism means the same few are repeatedly involved. Both the police and the schools are on the alert for signs of gang activity. Although this has not been a major problem, it tends to surface at the start of each new school year, and authorities recognize that living in a small town does not provide immunity to big city problems. Officials point to lack of communication and understanding between the youths of the newcomers and the host population as the main cause of interracial problems. Violent activity also takes place between youths of the minority groups themselves. Authorities in Mountain Lake note that Laotians of that city do not cause problems on "their own turf." The problems come from outside gangs. In Mountain Lake parents are cooperative with law enforcement officials, and the Laotian community quickly steps in to handle the problems of its own people.

In St. James, Hispanic newcomers are just beginning to become homeowners. The few who lived there before the large influx had already bought homes, but it has only been recently that more newly arrived Hispanics have become homeowners.

The Laotian community in Mountain Lake places a high priority on home ownership. Several members of an extended family will live in one house until enough money can be saved to purchase another. They try to be good neighbors and learn what is expected of them in the way of home and yard care.

Civic, school, and church leaders in both St. James and Mountain Lake report that the host community, for the most part, accepts the new minorities. Some people reject them, however, while others are simply indifferent. In both towns the minorities primarily associate with their own group. The Laotians "seem to have a party every weekend, all weekend long," according to one Mountain Lake resident.

There are important differences between Hispanics in St. James and Laotians in Mountain Lake. Most Hispanics come to St. James (and other southwestern Minnesota communities) from "the Valley" in Texas. They have family there, and often return to their family for months at a time. This leaves them with less incentive to learn English and make St. James home.

The Laotians, on the other hand, come from Laos by way of California, the Twin Cities, Iowa, or Nebraska. They come as refugees from a country whose repressive government does not allow them to return home. Therefore, they are more apt to view Mountain Lake as their home. Becoming American citizens is a high priority for them.

Whether the immigrants come to southwestern Minnesota for a temporary job or to make a permanent home, the leaders of the host communities of St. James and Mountain Lake recognize the newcomers as important members of their communities. Without them their communities would decline.

Madelia

Madelia's civic leaders know what they are doing. They know they need minorities, Mexicans and Mexican Americans, for their town to have any future at all. They do not look at the 50 percent Hispanic first grade as a matter to contest but as a fact that they must affirm, even though, in truth, leaders of town and school have not worked out a curriculum or school plan that would enhance full participation and mutual understanding.

The leaders know their numbers. They have the 1990 census at hand. Some things were not good. Although its percentage of unemployed in the decade had gone from 6 percent to 4 percent, the percentage of residents below the poverty level went from 6 to 15 percent. Nevertheless, things could have been worse. After all, in the 1980s Madelia grew from 2,130 to 2,237, while the agricultural county around it had decreased from 12,361 to 11,682. Its median age went down from 37.6 years to 35.9 years. Its average household size, a sign of children, rose slightly from 2.43 persons to 2.47 persons. Its total housing rose from 892 units to 923 units, its rental vacancies dropped from 8 to 7, and the median value of its housing units increased from $34,000 to $37,000.

In St. James, a notch above Madelia, the median value of housing went from $36,600 to $36,700, while the state jumped from $54,300 to $74,000. The town's median rent increased from $131 to $202. Median household income rose from $14,500 to $20,700. Most significant of all for the town's immediate future, school enrollment increased from 360 to 493. Presently, the elementary school is 30 percent Hispanic; the high school is 16 percent. A further comparison of these two communities appears in the following charts.

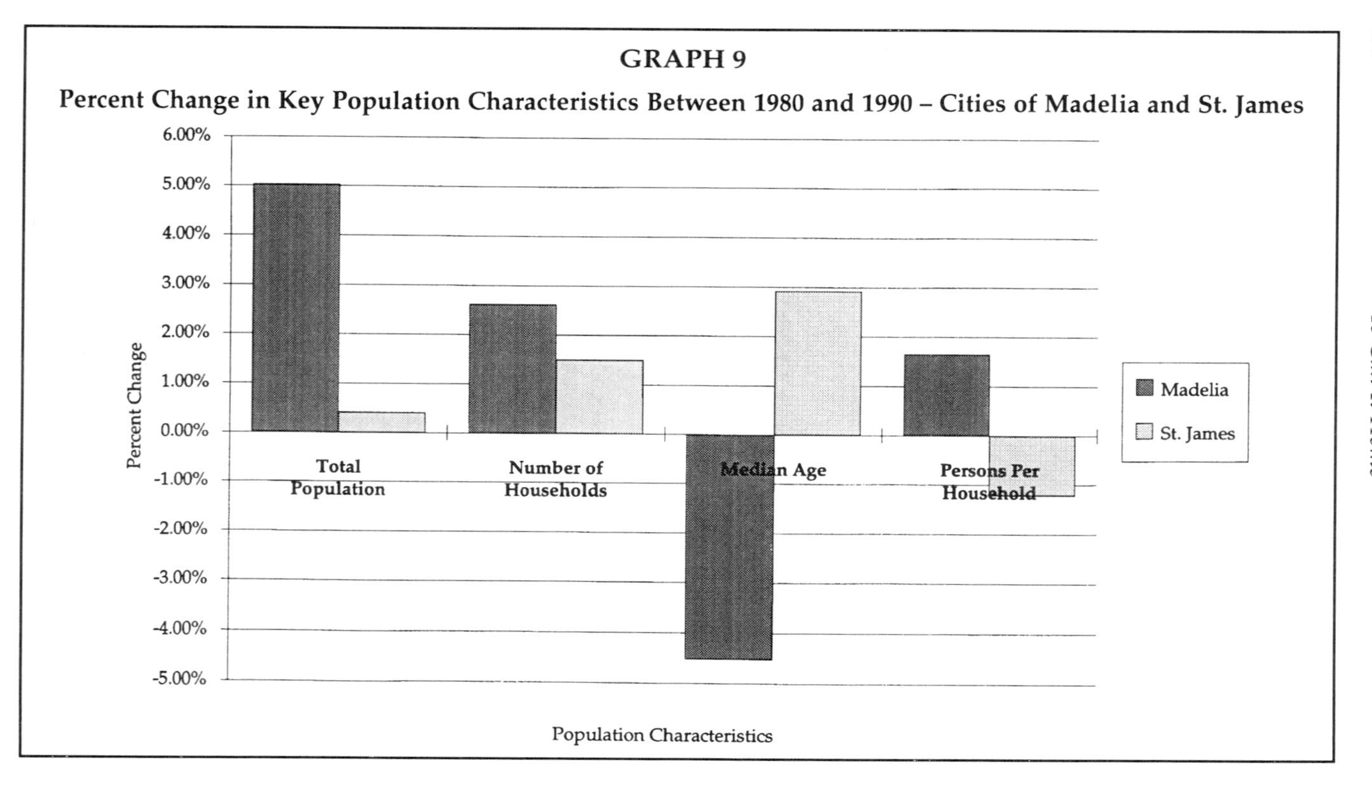
GRAPH 9
Percent Change in Key Population Characteristics Between 1980 and 1990 – Cities of Madelia and St. James
6.00%
5.00%
4.00%
3.00%
2.00%
1.00%
0.00%
-1.00%
-2.00%
-3.00%
-4.00%
-5.00%
Percent Change
Total Population
Number of Households
Median Age
Persons Per Household
Madelia
St. James
Population Characteristics

GRAPH 10

Percent Change in Key Socio-Economic Characteristics Between 1980 and 1990 – Cities of Madelia and St. James

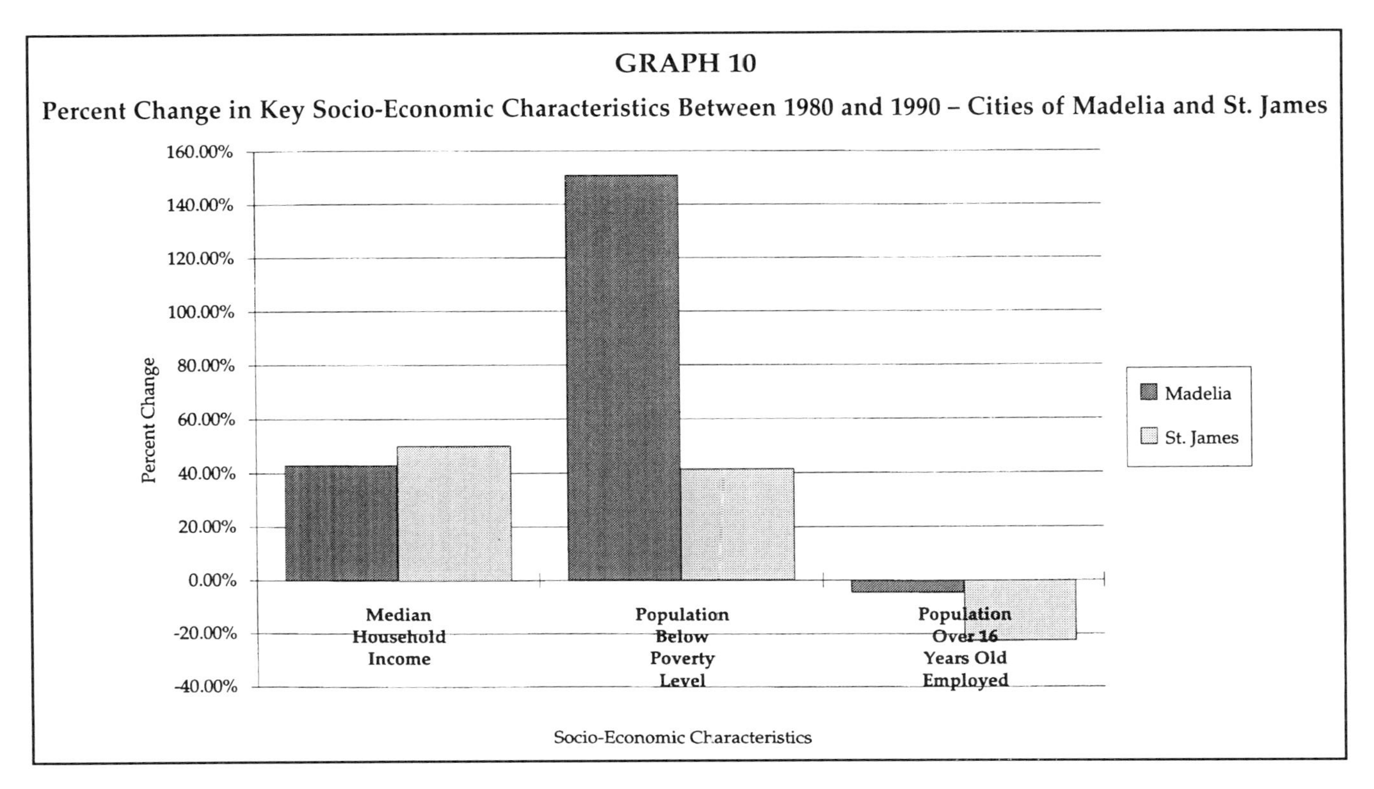

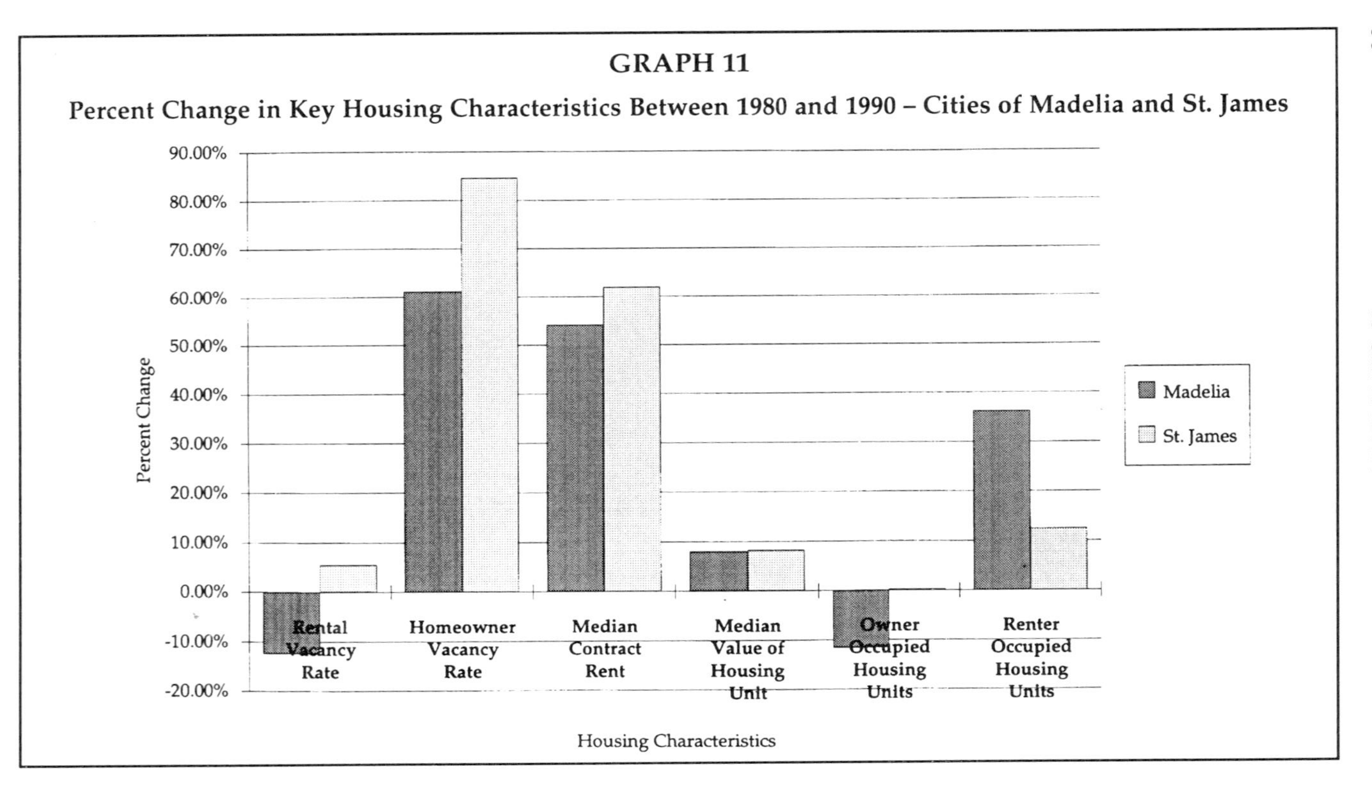

GRAPH 11

Percent Change in Key Housing Characteristics Between 1980 and 1990 – Cities of Madelia and St. James

Madelia's growth did not come from the surrounding area. In fact, its service area had grown smaller and contracted in recent history. No push of population outward from the Twin Cities or Mankato increased Madelia. Instead what made the difference was the expansion of its own long-established food-processing industry, Tony Downs, and food-processing plants in surrounding towns. The new minorities the industries brought in as well as Madelia's available and affordable housing made a good match. Madelia's Hispanic population increased from 81 to 198 in the 1980s, and the Hispanic population is predicted to double again by the end of the century.

The leaders now sense that the great period of turbulence is behind them. The days of rapid expansion are over. Numbers at the community food shelf indicate how families have fared in Madelia. The food shelf went from serving 900 single males in 1991 to serving 205 adults and 165 children in 1993. The newcomers are willing to call law enforcement officials, who have learned to understand new customs and ways and now avoid making children their parents' interpreters. The local industry helped pay for an English program for the newcomers. There is a small summer festival. The bank has even translated some of its materials into Spanish. There is considerable pride in the park which was built so it would be accessible to the newcomers. The leaders are proud of the way they have worked together, although they acknowledge that they still have much work to do with the school.

Yet the candor of Madelia reveals a certain longing for a community promised but not realized. They do not feel they have entered into close contact with the newcomers. One Catholic woman, who wanted to share her common Catholic faith with them, regretfully said, "Few of them go to church. They don't use church the way we do." There is still considerable suspicion and finger-pointing at the newcomers. At times children from the host community taunt the Hispanic children (even those who are children of U.S. citizens and mixed marriages): "Go home, you illegal!" Several leaders were disappointed that their attempts to organize renters in the trailer court failed. They could not form an alliance between residents and newcomers even when they shared a common interest in action. Some residents think that there is violence in their schools and neighboring schools, and some parents may be considering the use of alternative schools. At a meeting between the author and Madelia representatives, one Mexican American, married to a long-term resident woman, who himself had lived in Madelia several years, contended, with long and deeply pent-up pain, that he remains invisible to fellow residents. He asserted that he and his children would remain outsiders in Madelia no matter how many years he stays, and that Mexicans will always remain immigrants and the embodiment of immigrants no matter whoever else comes and goes. He felt things had gotten worse in the last five years.

In Madelia it is clear that the road to remaking a community is not easy, even with the best intentions of leaders who perceive their newcomers as part of the hope of their town's future. It is not easy for people launched in life along such different trajectories to call the same place home and to include one another in the community of heart and understanding.

Yet the collection of leaders gathered in Madelia in February 1996 seemed convincingly committed to being open, fair, and determined to stay the course. They included the mayor, the city administrator, a police officer, a telephone company employee, the food shelf director, the chamber of commerce representative, a banker, two members of the school board, two Mexican community organizers, and a mixed race couple. They all agreed that they had come a long way from the tumult and turbulence of just a few years before, but they acknowledge that they still have a long way to go to make Madelia home for all.

Montevideo and Willmar

On April 26, 1995, a groundbreaking ceremony took place in Montevideo, Minnesota. In a surprisingly well-advertised event, Minnesota Governor Arne Carlson and two members of the local chamber of commerce joined the founder and the president of Jennie-O Foods in launching the construction of a $14 million poultry-processing plant. For city and county leaders, the start of construction marked the successful conclusion of a lengthy effort to attract the poultry processor. In exchange for the 150 new jobs planned by Jennie-O Foods, Chippewa County donated 20 acres of land, a nine-ton road, and $60,000 in sewer and water assessments.[1] Anticipation of the 1996 opening ran high.

Local leaders had courted Jennie-O as an "economic enhancement" and an answer to the county's decline.[2] The plant in Montevideo was an expansion designed to handle spillover from its operations in Willmar, a regional hub some thirty miles to the east. Company officials had concluded that Willmar, the city where Jennie-O Foods was founded in 1949, simply could not meet the needs of their industry's most recent cycle of growth.[3] By enthusiastically opening their community to Jennie-O, city and county leaders joined the ranks of a number of other small-town leaders who placed their hopes in a new industry.

---

[1]Pat Schmidt, "Gov. Carlson flies in for groundbreaking," *Montevideo American-News* 27 April 1995, 3A.

[2]Ibid.

[3]See Forrest Peterson, "As Willmar grows, so do challenges," *West Central Tribune* (Willmar, Minn. Hereafter, *WCT*) 19 June 1995, 10A.

The story of Jennie-O in Montevideo and Willmar is about a lot more than hope in growth or industry. Roughly ten months after the groundbreaking ceremony, an article appeared in the Montevideo newspaper titled "Prepare for Jennie-O Influx with knowledge; law enforcement have had special training."[4] The reporter described the city's last-minute preparations for Jennie-O with the following lines from a meeting: "Speak out. Refute racist comments. Learn conversational Spanish. Educate yourself on other cultures."[5] Locals, familiar with Jennie-O's operation in Willmar, assumed expansion in Montevideo would mean the arrival of newcomers—in this case, "Mexicans."[6] Despite the fact that only about 25 percent of Jennie-O's Willmar employees in 1993 were Hispanic, Willmar, poultry processing, and "Mexicans" have blended together in conversations across southwestern Minnesota.[7] The growth of the Hispanic population has coincided with the rise of the poultry industry, and nowhere in southwestern Minnesota has this population been as visible as in Willmar.

In trying to make sense of their future, Montevideo's leaders looked to Willmar as a model. With a population slightly less than 20,000, Willmar, the seat of Kandiyohi County, is the largest city in southwestern Minnesota. In contrast to Montevideo, which is anticipating the arrival of its first year-round Hispanic population, Willmar's recent experience with new people and new economic trends reaches back more than a decade. In the late 1980s, a sizable influx of new arrivals took place. Between 1980 and 1990, the Hispanic population in Willmar grew by 750 percent. Some recent estimates place the

---

[4]See *Montevideo American-News* 15 February 1996, 2A.
[5]Ibid.
[6]The majority of Willmar's new arrivals are actually from the United States. Willmar also has a small, but significant group of residents who trace their roots to other parts of Latin America.
[7]Gregg Aamot, "Jennie-O Foods successful in hiring Hispanics," *WCT* 8 June 1993; and Susan Green, "Del Valle a Willmar: Settling out of the Migrant Stream in a Rural Minnesota Community," Julian Samora Research Institute Working Paper #19 May 1994, p. 6.

population at over 10 percent of the city's total population or slightly more than 2,000.[8]

Willmar's Hispanic population has its roots in a migrant tradition. By the 1950s, seasonal migrations to southern Minnesota, which date back to the turn of the century, were firmly established. Every summer, migrants mainly from the Rio Grande Valley in Texas would journey northward to work in the fields of Kandiyohi County and neighboring Renville County. In the middle of the 1980s, the flow of migrants into the region intensified.[9] Changes at both the southern and the northern ends of the migration stream were responsible for the new intensity. The Mexican economic crisis, epitomized by Mexico's spiraling inflation, forced many in the country to reconsider their options, and the mid-decade collapse in oil prices deflated the once-booming economy of Texas. Against the backdrop of the economic downturn in the American Southwest, the long-distance, seasonal journeys to southwestern Minnesota seemed more attractive. Growing labor shortages in southwestern Minnesota opened opportunities for permanent employment. The $6- to $7-an-hour starting wages in the poultry industry far exceeded anything available in Texas, where the economic downturn had made even minimum-wage jobs scarce. These opportunities led many migrants to choose to stay on in Willmar past the summer. By 1988, a large year-round resident population had developed out of the traditional stream of seasonal migrants.[10]

---

[8]See Gregg Aamot in *WCT* 27 January 1995, 1A; and Green, "Del Valle a Willmar," p. 2.

[9]Green, pp. 4–6; and David Little, "Migrants fill seasonal labor need," *WCT* 24 August 1987, 1A, 2A, 10A. "Studies chart trends in number of U.S. Hispanics," *WCT* 26 August 1987, 3A.

[10]Ibid.; Anne Polta, "Many Hispanics work their way off public assistance," *WCT* 1 June 1993, 10A; Sharon Bomstad, "Assistance available for Hispanics in area," *WCT* 25 August 1987, 3A, 6A; and Interview with James Kulset and Julie Asmus. These observations are supported by the life stories of local families and individuals drawn from national and local papers. The Life History Corpus in this report assembles information from the following articles: "Being Hispanic: What's it mean," *WCT* 6 May 1993, 1A, 8A; Gregg Aamot, "Schooled for Success: Hispanics finding skills and jobs through Willmar Technical College," *WCT* 18 May 1993, 1A, 6A; Debbie Howlett,

Since then, employment among the city's permanent Hispanic population has remained closely tied to Jennie-O. Although Hispanic residents are now employed in various service sector jobs, the majority of them have not found jobs elsewhere in Willmar above entry-level positions. They have found a degree of horizontal mobility in the region (usually from poultry processing to retail sales), but unfortunately this mobility involves trading one set of less-than-ideal conditions for another. Workers who choose to look outside of Jennie-O must almost invariably accept less pay and fewer hours.

Hispanic residents' incomes reflect the lack of sufficient opportunities beyond the entry level. According to the 1990 Census, Willmar had a per capita income of $11,481 in 1989, while the city's Hispanic population had a per capita income of $3,254 during the same period.[11] The census revealed an even greater gap in incomes between the city's non-Hispanic and Hispanic populations. Even when the trend among Hispanics to have larger households is taken into account (a nationwide average of 3.6 persons per household among Hispanics versus an average of 1.9 among the U.S. population as a whole), Hispanic incomes lag behind the incomes of Willmar's non-Hispanic population.[12] Whether framed in terms of individuals or households, a sharp disparity in incomes exists between Willmar's Hispanic residents and the

---

"Midwest new hub for Hispanics," *USA Today* 15 December 1995; Gregg Aamot, "Jennie-O Foods successful in hiring Hispanics," *WCT* 8 June 1993; Idem, "Education is key to success," *WCT* 7 July 1993; Ibid., in *WCT* 27 January 1995, 1A; Rand Middleton, "For Hispanics, education is a key to success," *WCT* 27 August 1987, 3A, 7A; Joan Wright, "Migrant worker tells his family's story," *WCT* 29 August 1987, 3A, 8A; David Little, "Hispanic students find success," *WCT* 8 May 1993, 1A, 2A; Gary Miller, "Hispanic alliance honors employees," *WCT* 20 September 1994; Idem, "Family finds cooperation and determination can open doors to new home," *WCT* 20 June 1995, 10A; Ibid., 20 February 1995; Ibid., 15 June 1995, 10A.; and Pat Doyle, "Willmar barrio on brink: Residents face eviction they say they can't afford," *Star Tribune* (Minneapolis) 5 February 1995, 1A.

[11]1990 Census of Population and Housing, Summary Tape File 3A, Minnesota, Willmar city and Per Capita Income.

[12]See Steve Gravelle, "Experts differ on the size of the state's Hispanic population," *WCT* 26 August 1987.

rest of the population. In their starkest form, these laggard incomes mean poverty. In contrast to Kandiyohi County's non-Hispanic population, 13 percent of whom lived in poverty in 1990, 68 percent of the county's Hispanic population fell below the poverty line.[13]

This poverty, which constitutes an enormous obstacle for the new residents, is particularly troubling when it is viewed within the framework of mobility. Pulling oneself out of poverty has never been easy, but Willmar's newcomers appear to have had a noticeably harder time than many other recent American immigrants. Census figures demonstrate that recent immigrants to the United States achieve parity in household income approximately ten years after their arrival.[14] The disparity of incomes in Willmar points to a disturbing trend. Although some may dismiss this, arguing that less than ten years elapsed between the 1990 Census and the Hispanic population's arrival in Willmar in the mid- to late-1980s, a deeper inquiry into the disparity of incomes establishes cause for concern. The vast majority of Willmar's Hispanic population resided in the United States for several years prior to their arrival in Willmar. Some lived in Texas for over a decade prior to venturing north, and are not actually immigrants, but American-born U.S. citizens.[15] The existence of the income gap can be accounted for by three explanations. First, the opportunities offered in Willmar—and other small cities as well—are insufficient to provide parity, and the immigrants who do achieve parity do so only by leaving the region. Second, those who have migrated tend to have experienced more troubles than others in finding favorable opportunities. In fact, their arrival in Willmar is a part of a long string of attempts to bet-

---

[13]Anne Polta, "Many Hispanics work their way off public assistance," *WCT* 1 June 1993.

[14]See Linda Chavez and John J. Miller, "The Immigration Myth," *Reader's Digest*, May 1996, p. 72.

[15]See Gary Miller, "Local Officials say *USA Today* article on Willmar was fair," *WCT* 19 December 1995, 1A. Along similar lines, according to census figures, only 11 percent of all Hispanics in Minnesota are not citizens. (See Ibid.) See the Life History Corpus.

ter their lot. Finally, the income gap stems from endemic poverty in rural areas and small cities.

Leaders of the host community are not oblivious to the challenges that new residents confront. In explaining the new residents' poverty and mobility, they have been quick to cite the immigrants' lack of education and their inadequate knowledge of English as the major stumbling blocks in their efforts to get ahead. Nevertheless, a number of statistics challenge the image of Willmar's Hispanic population as uneducated and non-English speaking. Most do speak English. Though less educated than their non-Hispanic counterparts, not all Hispanic residents are poorly educated. According to the 1990 Census, 35 percent of Willmar's Hispanic population 25 and older possessed a high school diploma or the equivalent, and 17 percent had some training beyond high school.[16] Furthermore, some have served in the United States Armed Forces.[17] Clearly, language and education alone do not adequately explain the new arrivals' poverty.

Willmar's resident Hispanic population retains migrant characteristics. Mirroring the migrants who still come for two months out of the year, many of the city's Hispanics come for two or three years and then depart. A constant influx of new arrivals replenishes their population. Employers, social service providers, and educators have all noted substantial turnover in the Hispanic community. This turnover raises questions about their future in the region. Even though many attain $7- or $8-an-hour jobs, new arrivals have other ideas of advancement, especially when it comes to their children's prospects for a better future. As early as 1987, observers noted a trend among younger Hispanics in south-central Minnesota to move to the Twin Cities area.[18] Ultimately, new residents'

---

[16]1990 Census of Population and Housing, Summary Tape File 3A, Minnesota, Willmar city and educational attainment. These numbers are higher than those for the state's Hispanic population as a whole. Roughly one in four Hispanics has a high school diploma, and 15 percent hold a bachelor's degree. See Wendy S. Tai, "A Frosty Welcome," *Star Tribune* 3 June 1994, 1A.
[17]See the Life History Corpus.
[18]Steve Gravelle, "Experts differ on the size of the state's Hispanic population," *WCT* 26 August 1987.

willingness to stay in Willmar will depend on the city's industry and its ability to offer them upward mobility.

Despite poverty and high turnover, some trends indicate change. Recently, Hispanic employees have begun to appear in new workplaces, ranging from Rice Memorial Hospital to the school system.[19] Expansion into new sectors of the economy has deepened Hispanic roots in the region—roots that can serve as the basis for future mobility. In its growing economy, Willmar counts several Hispanic-owned businesses, including a grocery store, a restaurant, and an auto repair shop.[20] Willmar's Hispanic population has also been making use of local higher-education institutions. During the 1992–93 school year, the technical college and the community college each enrolled several dozen Hispanic students. During the 1990–91 and 1992–93 school years, the technical college produced eighteen Hispanic graduates. Of these eighteen, eight have found employment in Willmar businesses.[21] In sum, there is no shortage of success stories among Willmar's Hispanic community, which includes a small but growing group of professionals.[22]

When put in a larger historical context, these trends point to the future emergence of a permanent and secure Hispanic population. In the mid-1980s, the region's Hispanics were overwhelmingly migrants involved in seasonal agricultural labor. Today, even though field work continues to provide a source of income for many households (especially for minors who contribute by working in the fields), a substantial non-agricultural population has grown out of the streams of migrants. The increasing tendency toward long-term settlement indicates that many recent arrivals believe that, at least for now, Willmar is their best option.[23]

At times, the promise of this progress has been shadowed.

---

[19]See Ibid., and the Interview with James Kulset and Julie Asmus in note #10.

[20]See the Life History Corpus, and Green, "Del Valle a Willmar," p. 10.

[21]Gregg Aamot, "Schooled for Success: Hispanics finding skills and jobs through Willmar Technical College," *WCT* 18 May 1993, 1A.

[22]See the Life History Corpus.

[23]A number of individuals echoed this conclusion. See the Life History Corpus.

The new arrivals' difficulties have been compounded by negative images of Hispanics. They have confronted stereotypes that portray them as lazy, less intelligent, and predisposed to crime and violence. These stereotypes have been at the core of charges of discrimination. Some Hispanics have accused local branches of the Minnesota Department of Jobs and Training of automatically referring all Hispanics to Jennie-O—even those who are well trained and educated.[24] Also, the State Human Rights Commission has registered allegations of discrimination in hiring and firing, and some of its findings have supported these allegations.[25]

In addition to the workplace, education and law enforcement have become the focal points of allegations as well. Two well-publicized lawsuits alleging discrimination have captured headlines. In July 1992, Arturo Dearo, a Willmar police officer from El Paso, Texas, filed suit against the city, alleging that fellow officers had routinely subjected him to unfair treatment and harassment. Roughly two months later, Dearo, who had received anonymous threats, discovered an imitation grenade had been placed in his car. (A subsequent internal investigation described the incident as an accident stemming from a prank played on another officer.) In December 1992, the city settled the lawsuit brought by Dearo, paying him $75,000 in exchange for his resignation.[26] Formal allegations have not been confined to the Dearo case. In a class-action lawsuit filed in U.S. District Court in Minneapolis on March 7, 1996, thirteen Hispanic families alleged that the Willmar School District segregated Hispanic children. Still unsettled as of June 1996, the lawsuit claims that Hispanic children, who comprise approximately 20 percent of the district's students, were routinely placed in English as a Second Language classes even when they came from English-speaking households.[27] Many local

[24]See Gary Miller in *WCT* 12 December 1994, 1A; and Green, "Del Valle a Willmar," p. 6.

[25]See "Ruling backs racism charge," *WCT* 15 March 1996, 1A.

[26]Kurt Chandler, "Hispanic officer resigns," *Star Tribune* 24 December 1992, 1A; and Green, "Del Valle a Willmar," p. 12.

[27]Gary Miller, "Hispanic families file class-action lawsuit against school district," *WCT* 8 March 1996, 1A.

leaders who have striven to serve the Hispanic community felt blind-sided by the suit, whose origin they locate outside the community.

A persistent housing shortage has produced tension in Willmar as well.[28] The housing shortage has been exacerbated by bad timing. The unexpected influx of employment-seeking arrivals came precisely at a time when the housing market was weakened in its capacity to expand and absorb new entrants. In the early 1980s, high interest rates and a farm crisis produced a slump in new housing starts, and through the late 1980s, construction of new housing failed to keep pace with the growth of the population. When the newcomers began to flow into the city in the late 1980s, they quickly discovered that the availability of affordable housing was limited. However, builders and landlords have hesitated to invest in housing for a population whom they view as less than ideal tenants—low-income and temporary.[29]

With few options in this market, many of the new arrivals moved to the Elm Lane Mobile Home Park. In 1990, almost half of the city's Hispanic population resided there. The trailer park became a microcosm of the problems that arose out of the city's housing shortage and rapid growth. According to the police department, Elm Lane generated more "calls than any other neighborhood in the city."[30] The troubles at Elm Lane prompted the police department to set up a substation at the entrance to the trailer park. Everyone who entered or exited the park was required to check in or out at the post.[31] In the span of less than two years in 1994 and 1995, several shootings took place in the park, including the August 1994 fatal shoot-

---

[28]See Polta in *WCT* 1 June 1993; Gregg Aamot, "Groups working to help residents," *WCT* 14 November 1994, 1A; Forrest Peterson, "As Willmar grows, so do challenges," *WCT* 19 June 1995, 10A.

[29]One recent article suggested that developers in Montevideo might be leaning toward the "high end" as well. See *Montevideo American-News* 27 April 1996, 3A.

[30]Doyle, "Willmar barrio on brink," 1A.

[31]Green, "Del Valle a Willmar," p. 14; and Interview with James Kulset and Julie Asmus in note #10.

ing of Jesus Molina. Elm Lane's problems attracted attention from across the state.[32]

Elm Lane pitted city leaders, the park's owner, and residents against each other. In 1989, the city passed an ordinance requiring that all mobile home parks conform to a set of minimum standards for density, access, and fire lanes. The council gave William Begin, the owner of Elm Lane, five years to bring the park into compliance. When the deadline expired on July 1, 1994, Begin's efforts had fallen short of the council's requirements. Prior to the July 1 deadline, rumors had circulated among the park's residents that the city was planning a mass eviction. Realizing that closing the park would result in substantial displacement, city leaders offered a compromise to Begin, accepting his plans to widen the streets by two feet.[33] The agreement was short-lived; in October, Begin announced that he would be closing the park on July 31, 1995. During the next nine months, city leaders and community activists floated different proposals.[34] As the deadline approached and no solution appeared, accusations of racism and indifference flew.[35] Despite a last-minute flurry of negotiations and litigation, the city shut off the water to the trailer park on August 1, 1995. A court order allowed residents to stay past the shut-off until the end of the month. In August 1995, the last residents of Elm Lane departed.[36]

The closing of Elm Lane raised many issues. In the months leading up to the closing, residents' legal counsel argued that each household should receive a sum ranging from $1,000 to $3,000 from Begin for relocation costs. Even though city officials chose to exercise their authority under a Minnesota law that allowed them to hold Begin liable for residents' relocation costs, the city council set sums ranging from $150 to $400 for

---

[32]Doyle, "Willmar barrio on brink," 1A.

[33]Mark Shores in *WCT* 21 June 1994.

[34]Gregg Aamot, "Groups working to help residents," *WCT* 14 November 1994, 1A; Gary Miller, "70 families still looking for housing," *WCT* 27 February 1996; Idem, "HUD official calls Willmar efforts toward Elm Lane commendable," *WCT* 9 February 1995, 1A.

[35]Ibid.

[36]*Star Tribune*, 19 July 1995, 2B; and *Star Tribune*, 4 August 1995, 7B.

each eligible resident.[37] A Kandiyohi County judge sided with the council's assessments, and residents received sums well below what they had requested.

Although the Elm Lane discussions revolved around specific sums of money, they took on a decidedly moral tone. Notifying city officials of his decision to close the park, Begin said he had grown "weary of being a 'one-man low-income housing authority.'"[38] Several city officials argued that the city had no obligation to make good on a landlord's failure to deliver on his promises. Others argued that the city had a moral responsibility to take measures to protect vulnerable members of the community. Community activists alleged that the city had used the whole process to rid itself of an eyesore and to duck out of obligations to its citizens. The whole episode highlighted what they saw as a philosophy of callous exploitation: City fathers, they said, had welcomed the new residents as a source of revenue and cheap labor, but when the newcomers turned to them for help, city fathers responded with talk of limited liability and self-reliance.[39] The debate over Elm Lane raised a difficult question: Who should pay for the new residents' housing?

The Elm Lane crisis forced the city to address issues affecting its Hispanic population. The crisis demonstrated to city, county, and state leaders that they could not afford to ignore problems in housing, education, and the workplace. Many local leaders who had earlier watched from a safe distance began to take more active roles in the lives of the new residents. Where once a "wait-and-see" attitude toward new arrivals had prevailed, attitudes based on a sense of a shared future emerged. Civic groups, charitable associations, and private industry created a million-dollar fund to help former Elm

---

[37]See Doyle, "Willmar barrio on brink," 1A.

[38]Richard Meryhew, "Park residents appeal to Willmar for relocation help," *Star Tribune* 19 January 1995, 5B.

[39]See Gary Miller, "Federal Probe into Elm Lane," *WCT* 24 January 1995, 1A; Idem, *WCT* 6 February 1995, 1A; Idem, *WCT* 20 February 1995; Meryhew, "Park residents appeal to Willmar," 5B; and Doyle, "Willmar barrio on brink," 1A.

Lane residents find housing. The Community Activity Set Aside Program (CASA, which means "home" in Spanish) has provided qualified residents with first mortgage loans at 4.8 percent. (Helping families become homeowners has required an extra effort. In one case, a realtor followed up with a referral; a banker went out of his way to help prepare a difficult application; and a local church provided the down payment.)[40]

Despite Willmar's problems, civic leaders, neighboring communities, and new residents can benefit by reflecting on their successes which have come from Willmar's investments in its citizens. Given this history, newcomers cannot be viewed merely as a source of income and labor; they require similar investments as well. As part of this process, long-time residents of Willmar will have to accustom themselves to a new class of Hispanic professionals. They will encounter them not just as equals, but as colleagues, associates, peers, and even superiors. The opportunities found in a regional health care, education, and government center must extend to the whole population. Willmar cannot expect these new arrivals to remain if the region fails to live up to its commitments. Even Willmar, the city with the largest Hispanic community in the region, could become just one stop in a larger migration which spans generations, classes, and continents.

In conclusion, both mature Willmar and newcomer Montevideo challenge prevailing images of rural Minnesota. Minnesotans, who have become accustomed to referring to the rural areas of their state with adjectives such as "lily-white," "white-bread," and "colorless," should reconsider their views. For the past two decades, paralleling national trends, a "browning" of the state's labor force has taken place, further calling into question the age-old clichés about ethnic homogeneity and uniformity in rural Minnesota. In areas where European immigrants and their descendants once prevailed, a new flow of immigrants from Mexico and the American

[40]Gary Miller, "Programs available to help people find affordable housing," and "Family finds cooperation and determination can open doors to new home," *WCT* 20 June 1995, 10A.

Southwest is opening a new chapter in the ongoing story of ethnic change in the region. The stories of Willmar and Montevideo should serve as starting points for those who wish to understand rural Minnesota and its new populations.

Conclusion

Our recommendations repeat suggestions found, at least implicitly, throughout this report.

First, our advice to leaders is moral: Recognize newcomers as fellow pilgrims, deserving all the justice, fairness, and respect we wish our own immigrant ancestors would have received.

Second, leaders should supplement moral sentiment with knowledge. They should recognize that newcomers are different from one another; they have different backgrounds and goals; and they follow different strategies and trajectories in the search for a place to call home. Although they live here, they remain emotionally, socially, and economically attached to distant places where family and friends remain.

The newcomers do not see themselves in terms of abstract classifications of race, continent, or even nation. Their primary identities are about families, clans, villages, regions, and work. The newcomers, at least in most instances, have not brought with them an elite (leaders, priests, intellectuals, newspaper editors, etc.) who define them as a group and constitute leadership for the new community equivalent to that of the host community. The newcomers' leadership involves and displays itself in more basic forms than the public affairs that concern the leaders of the host community.

Leaders of the host community should recognize that, however kindly and fairly they treat newcomers, even prolonged residency in one place does not mean the newcomers will consider it home. Like immigrants everywhere, they may treat their immediate location (however long they remain) as only a matter of temporary necessity or advantage.

Furthermore, even the newcomers who become permanent residents and wish to become U.S. citizens may not wish to be assimilated. Having lost a homeland, they may strive, above all else, not to lose their children and community to a new land and its new ways. Immigrants work hardest at recreating a better version of the world they left behind. They seek the advantages of the new world while keeping the values, sentiments, and traditions of the old. In any case, leaders should recognize that the newcomers alone will decide when they finally call a place home.

Leaders should join a general understanding of migrants and immigrants with a precise knowledge of community newcomers. They should seek to know who exactly the newcomers are. It is especially important to understand their composition, migration patterns, hopes, and goals. They should know the most recent data regarding housing, law enforcement, and social services, making careful distinctions between the first six months to one year after arrival and continuing residency, so they can protect new immigrants against stereotypes associating them collectively with crime, welfare exploitation, and abuse of residency.

Understanding what newcomers experience daily at work and in the streets, stores, and schools is yet another goal. Local leaders need a grasp of what people, especially the working class and new minorities, encounter day-in and day-out and what they worry about most. This knowledge, which should be actively sought, must be systematically brought to the attention of other community leaders, particularly teachers. This knowledge will strengthen leaders' abilities to help minority newcomers in particular, and their own working and laboring classes in general.

Leaders should also take measure of how newcomers are taking root in their community. They must try to judge whether a significant number of newcomers are choosing to settle there. Newcomers who wish to stay will spread out in the work force. They will buy trailers and houses. With more families and fewer single males, there will be less violent crime associated with the newcomers, although concern for adolescent gangs and crime may emerge as a problem. Eventually, the children of the newcomers, turned residents, will perform as well as other children, and their attendance, participation, and graduation records will improve. Indeed, it is at the school that the community can best monitor the newcomers and seek the common ground of their children's good. Some of these signs are already appearing in our region.

As part of a continuing community profile (based on sound demographic and anthropological research), which we believe every community should develop, leaders must observe whether or not newcomers are taking root in their community. Such an annual, or bi-annual, profile could be made by calculating: (1) the number of families in town in contrast to single individuals; (2) the number of violent crimes which should proportionately decrease with a reduction of the number of single males; (3) the diffusion of the new group into the workplace; and (4) the renting of apartments and trailers as opposed to owning homes. The numbers of newcomers and minority children, their rate of transfer, attendance rate, and rate of participation in English as a Second Language, advanced courses, and extracurricular rates can be tracked with school data. Finally, graduation rates and rates of those pursuing continuing education would assure a final measure of their participation in the views and opportunities of society.

Of equal importance, host communities must have a realistic view of themselves, their own histories, ethnic heritages, and present status. They must know and express the fact that the community that receives the newcomers has a complex past filled with diversity. Benefits from knowledge of the newcomers are conditional on resident leaders belonging to a coherent group with shared goals. In addition to knowing what is happening, and what they wish to happen, leaders must candidly define who they are. Equally, leaders from throughout the region and within each community must collaborate, acknowledging when and how they are working at cross purposes with one another in their approaches to the newcomers.

Additionally, leaders must know the principal employers of the newcomers. They should cooperate with these employers in seeking to secure a more stable work force characterized by less turnover and more opportunities for its employees. Leaders should not hesitate to judge what sort of relationship they have with the town's major employers. They should not cringe from calculating the public funds that subsidize private companies. They should meet regularly with local industries to discuss matters of mutual interest and advantage, particularly mutual projects that turn newcomers into long-term residents.

Furthermore, leaders should argue about issues of housing, taxes, schools, and industrial zoning, and their impact on bringing and retaining newcomers. As much as most rural leaders wish growth for its own sake, they must weigh it against creating a town in which class divisions are spawned, migrancy dominates, social costs are high, and a sense of disorder prevails.

The decisive issue for leaders is to create a good town. A quality town must continuously attract or, even better, generate companies that pay good wages. This means wages sufficient to attract and maintain workers who can accumulate the means to own property and provide a good life for their families. Mere survival (having, for example, simply enough children to keep one's schools open) is not enough. Community leaders must make sure their towns are not reduced to being a staging area for peoples' migration and the profits of distant corporate headquarters. A policy that fails to develop good jobs and full amenities, especially for the advantage of children, will neither attract nor retain smart, ambitious, and active citizens. Real rural and regional leaders, who wish their towns to be the best, must themselves be nimble and quick.

Finally, the leaders, insofar as they have the power and opportunity (which rarely appear in perfect tandem), must reforge their communities. At every level, they must seek to increase participation in communities that yield tangible results. Activities that join members of the host community and newcomers—be they parades, festivals, or building housing—

are particularly important. Leaders miss a great occasion if they don't have their schools invite all students and parents to tell the stories of their rich and differing migrations, whether those migrations took place one year ago or one hundred years ago.

Leaders of separate communities and towns should join one another in sharing knowledge of their experiences, experiments, and hopes in inventing a new community. Residents and newcomers alike need to know they share a long and challenging journey toward a place they will both call home.

Appendix: Aid Programs for Newcomers and Others

State and federally mandated assistance is available to people of all races and nationalities. The help that first comes to mind is "welfare." Welfare encompasses programs such as Aid to Families with Dependent Children (AFDC), medical assistance (MA), and food stamps. All of these programs have income guidelines. In the case of AFDC, there are several other restrictions, such as requiring two-parent families to find a job in four weeks. If they have not found a job in that time, they are placed at non-profit work sites to work off their welfare check. In almost all cases of welfare assistance, recipients face a time limit after which they cannot receive benefits.

The Southwest Minnesota Private Industry Council (PIC) is funded with federal, state, county, and private dollars. It provides job training, placement, and career counseling for its clients. Participants eligible for AFDC will probably also qualify for STRIDE (Success Through Reaching Individual Development and Employment), a program that assists with job training and placement, and can also help clients with the costs of higher education or obtaining a GED, as well as providing support services such as day-care, transportation, rent, moving costs, and clothing.

Western Community Action (WESCAP) has several programs to assist people who meet its guidelines. Head Start is probably its best-known program. Head Start does what its name implies: giving economically disadvantaged children a head start in education so they can begin school on the same level as other children. The income guideline is 100 percent of poverty, and the child must be between three and five years old. If the child is handicapped, the parent's level of income can be higher. This program also provides translators for those who need them and aids young parents in finding adequate day-care for their children.

WESCAP can also provide funds for home weatherization and fuel assistance. It has programs to repair homes owned by low-income people and can give some assistance with loans to first-time homebuyers. The self-sufficiency department provides budget counseling. Transportation assistance is given on either income guidelines or age. People over 60 are asked only to give a donation for the ride.

Besides providing transportation for senior citizens, the federal government also has nutrition programs for the elderly. Even relatively small communities have senior centers where the elderly can receive meals on a donation basis. For the homebound, there is Meals on Wheels. According to Carol Moseng, WESCAP director, few minority seniors take advantage of these meals. When the Marshall meal site sponsored a "Spanish night" where Hispanic people prepared and served the food, however, it was quite well attended by the local Hispanics and non-Hispanics.

The Social Security office is another place a newcomer might look for help. People 65 and older, or the disabled, may be eligible for up to $470 a month in Supplemental Social Security Income (SSI). For a couple that qualifies, the amount can be as high as $687. There are, however, strict income and disability guidelines for this assistance.

On the other end of the spectrum is Community Health Services (CHS), whose main focus is children. The Women, Infants, and Children (WIC) program provides food vouchers for infants, children, and pregnant women. This program is also income-based and requires a demonstrated nutritional need. Well-child exams, given on a sliding-fee scale, include vision and hearing tests and nutritional assessments. Immunizations are $5 a shot or free if the parents cannot afford them. Prenatal visits by a nurse are also provided.

CHS provides home care and home health aides based on a sliding fee. Water testing, a service that is particularly needed in rural areas, is also available on a sliding-fee scale.

One of the few benefits available to new immigrants that is not available to the general public is cash assistance to refugees in the amount of $200 per person.

All of these programs are funded by either the state or federal government, and are subject to the priorities and restrictions set by Congress or the state legislatures. Allocations to these programs can be either reduced or terminated depending on the prevailing political sentiment, which causes great uncertainty for those who depend on such programs to survive.

Some of the assistance available to new minority groups in the region, as well as to all low-income people, is government funded but not mandated. One of the most important is English as a Second Language (ESL). There are also high school equivalency (GED) classes for those who want to earn their high school diploma; Adult Basic Education (ABE) classes, basic reading classes for adults who can't read; and Alternative High School for "at risk" students who find the usual methods of education unsuccessful. This program is partially funded by local school boards and is offered at their discretion. According to Wanda Ochocki, education coordinator for Marshall Public Schools, there are few, if any, school districts in Minnesota where these programs are not offered. By law these programs are not available to children under age 16.

Minnesota Extension Services has set up a network of advocates known as Community Connectors. These people are fluent in the languages of the newcomers and are familiar with the services available to them. They can assist the new immigrants with advocacy and translation. This help is available only in southwestern Minnesota counties. Community Connectors in the schools are funded by the school districts.

Extension Services also has a food and nutrition program

that provides nutrition education to low-income families. This is a federally funded part of the food-stamp program. According to Shirley Anderson-Porisch, Lyon County Extension educator, contrary to general perceptions, new minorities are not beating a path to the doors of welfare agencies. Most do not know about the programs, or do not see themselves as being eligible, thus the need for the Community Connectors.

An important aid for the newcomers is legal advocacy. These advocates, located in Willmar and Mankato, serve the poor of the region by providing free legal help to those who meet their income guidelines or who are over 60. The advocates give legal counsel for all legal problems (except criminal cases) including domestic and family questions, landlord-tenant disputes, and Immigration and Naturalization Service (INS) matters. The government, however, is considering restricting funding for this program, which would virtually end this assistance. In the Mankato office, over 20 percent of their clients are Hispanic, and six of the employees speak Spanish. Southeast Asians are less likely to use the services of these advocates. Most of the problems can be handled by phone, but the advocates will drive around the region if the situation requires. The work of the legal advocates is funded by the state and federal governments and by local lawyers, who work pro bono.

Bibliography

GENERAL WORKS ON IMMIGRATION

Anzovin, Steven. *The Problem of Immigration*. New York: H. W. Wilson, 1985.

Borjas, George J. "Immigrant Participation in the Welfare System," *Industrial and Labor Relations Review* 44 (1991): 195–211.

Briggs, Vernon M., and Stephen Moore, eds. *Still an Open Door?* Washington, D.C.: American University Press, 1994.

Clark, Rebecca L. "The Costs of Providing Public Assistance and Education to Immigrants," Washington, D.C.: Urban Institute, August 1994.

Clark, Rebecca L., Jeffrey S. Passel, Wendy N. Zimmerman, and Michael E. Fix. "Fiscal Impacts of Undocumented Aliens: Selected Estimates for Seven States," Washington, D.C.: Urban Institute, January 1995.

Dudley, William. *Immigration: Opposing Viewpoints*. San Diego: Greenhaven Press, 1990.

Passel, Jeffrey, and Rebecca Clark. "How Much Do Immigrants Really Cost? A Reappraisal of Huddle's 'The Cost of Immigrants,'" Urban Institute, Washington, D.C., February 1994.

Portes, Alejandro, and József Böröcz. "Contemporary Immigration: Theoretical Perspectives on Its Determinants and Modes of Incorporation," *International Migration Review* 23, no. 3 (Fall 1989): 606–30.

Portes, Alejandro, and Rubén G. Rumbaut. *Immigrant America: A Portrait*. Berkeley, Calif.: University of California Press, 1990.

Simon, Julian. "Immigrants, Taxes, and Welfare in the United States," *Population and Development Review* 10, no. 1 (March 1984): 55–69.

Taylor, J. Edward, Philip L. Martin, and Michael Fix, et al., "Poverty Amidst Prosperity: Immigration and the Changing Face of Rural California," paper presented at the conference, Immigration and the Changing Face of Rural America, Ames, Iowa, July 11–13, 1996.

Tienda, Marta, and Leif Jensen. "Immigration and Public Assistance Participation: Dispelling the Myth of Dependency, *Social Science Research*, no. 15 (1986): 372–400.

Vecoli, Rudolph J., ed. *Gale Encyclopedia of Multicultural America*. New York: Gale Research Inc., 1995, 1:xxii–xxiii.

Yans-McLaughlin, Virginia, ed. *Immigration Reconsidered: History, Sociology, Politics*. Oxford: Oxford University Press, 1990.

WORKS ON HISPANICS

Acuña, Rodolfo. *Occupied America: A History of Chicanos*, 3d ed. New York: Harper and Row, 1988.

Aponte, Robert, and Marcelo Siles. "Latinos in the Heartland: The Browning of the Midwest," Research Report 5. Lansing, Mich.: Julian Samora Research Institute, November 1994.

Chase, Richard A., Suzanne Zerger, and Lisa Sass. "Minnesota Latino Needs and Resources Assessment," St. Paul: Wilder Research Center, May 1995.

Englekirk, Allen, and Marguerite Marín. "Mexican Americans," in *Gale Encyclopedia of Multicultural America*, Rudolph J. Vecoli, ed. New York: Gale Research Inc., 1995, 2:905–39.

Garcia, Juan Ramon. "Midwest Mexicanos in the 1920s: Some Research Issues, Questions, and Directions." *Social Science Journal*, April 1982.

Green, Susan. "Del Valle a Willmar: Settling out of the Migrant Stream in a Rural Minnesota Community," Working Paper 19. Lansing, Mich.: Julian Samora Research Institute, May 1994.

Maril, Robert Lee. *The Poorest Americans: The Mexican Americans of the Lower Rio Grande Valley of Texas*. Notre Dame: Notre Dame University Press, 1989.

Saenz, Rogelio. "Latino Poverty in the Midwest: A County-Level Analysis," Research Report 9. Lansing, Mich.: Julian Samora Research Institute, University of Michigan, September 1994.

Stavans, Ilan. *The Hispanic Condition: Reflections on Culture and Identity in America*. New York: Harper, 1996.

Steiner, Stan. *La Raza: The Mexican Americans*. New York: Harper and Row, 1970.

WORKS ON ASIANS

Baer, Florence E. "'Give me . . . your huddled masses': Anti-Vietnamese Refugee Lore and the 'Image of Limited Good,'" *Western Folklore* XLI, No. 4 (October, 1982), pp. 275–91.

Egerstrom, Lee. "A New Lease on Life: Moving to Rural Areas for Jobs, Asian, African, and Hispanic Immigrant Groups are Rejuvenating Small Minnesota Towns," *St. Paul Pioneer Press*, Jan. 9, 1994, 1D.

Grey, Mark A. "The Failure of Iowa's Non-English-Speaking Employees Law: A Case Study of Patronage, Kinship and Migration in Storm Lake, Iowa," *High Plains Applied Anthropologist* 13, no. 2 (Fall 1993): 32ff.

"Hmong of Minnesota," *Star Tribune*, April 21, 1985, 29A–38A.

Mattison, Wendy, et al., eds. *Hmong Lives from Laos to La Crosse: Stories of Eight Hmong Elders*. La Crosse: The Pump House, 1994.

Olney, Douglas P., ed. *A Bibliography of the Hmong (Miao)*. Minneapolis: Center for Urban and Regional Affairs, 1981.

Suzukamo, Les. "Hmong Relocate to New Life in Rural Minnesota," *St. Paul Pioneer Press*, June 30, 1991, 1A, 3A.

WORKS ON SOMALIS

Chin, Richard. "Somalis Build New Future in Minnesota," *St. Paul Pioneer Press*, March 5, 1995, p. 2B.

Johnson, Krystal L. "A Root of the Tree: A Case Study of Immigrant Experience Among a Group of Somali Women." University of Wisconsin, Milwaukee, M.A. Thesis: Dept. of Sociology, 1996.

Putnam, Diana Briton, and Mohamood Cabdi Noor. *The Somalis: Their History and Culture.* Washington, D.C.: Refugee Service Center, Center for Applied Linguistics, 1993, 4–17.

IMMIGRANTS AND RURAL MINNESOTA

Amato, Joseph, and John Radzilowski. *A New College on the Prairie: Twenty-Five Years of Southwest State University.* Marshall, Minn.: Crossings Press, 1992.

Amato, Joseph. *The Decline of Rural Minnesota.* Marshall, Minn.: Crossings Press, 1993.

Amato, Joseph. *Servants of the Land: God, Family, and Farm, a Trinity of Belgian Economic Folkways in Southwestern Minnesota.* Marshall, Minn.: Crossings Press, 1990.

Borchert, John R. *America's Northern Heartland: An Economic and Historical Geography of the Upper Midwest.* Minneapolis: University of Minnesota Press, 1987.

Holmquist, June Drenning, ed. *They Chose Minnesota: A Survey of the State's Ethnic Groups.* St. Paul: Minnesota Historical Society Press, 1981.

Klauda, Paul, and Suzanne P. Kelly. "Minority Population is Changing [the] Face of [the] State," *Star Tribune*, Feb. 22, 1991, 1A.

Radzilowski, John. "Family Labor and Immigrant Success in a Polish-American Rural Community," *Polish American Studies* 51, no. 2 (Autumn 1994): 49–66.

———. *Out on the Wind: Poles and Danes in Lincoln County Minnesota, 1880–1905*. Marshall, Minn.: Crossings Press, 1995.

———. *Prairie Town: A History of Marshall, Minnesota, 1872–1997*. Marshall: Lyon County Historical Society, forthcoming, 1997.

WORKS ON MEAT-PACKING

Benson, Janet E. "Garden City: Meatpacking and Immigration to the High Plains." Paper given at the conference, Immigration and the Changing Face of Rural America, Ames, Iowa, July 11–13, 1996.

Gouveia, Lourdes, and Donald Stull. "IBP's Impact on Lexington, Nebraska: A Report to the Community," June 1, 1996.

Grey, Mark A. "Turning the Pork Industry Upside Down: Storm Lake's Hygrade Workforce and the Impact of the 1981 Plant Closure," *The Annuals of Iowa* 54 (Summer 1995): 244–59.

Rigert, Joe, and Richard Meryhew, "In the Meat Factories," *Star Tribune*, April 30, 1995, 1A, 11A–13A.

Stull, Donald J., et al., eds. *Any Way You Cut It: Meat Processing and Small-Town America*. Lawrence: University Press of Kansas, 1995.

About the Authors

JOSEPH AMATO

Joseph Amato is Director of Regional Studies and a professor of history at Southwest State University in Marshall, Minnesota. He is an active member of the Society for the Study of Local and Regional History, and spurred many of its publications. The many books and articles authored by Professor Amato testify to his dedication to, and keen interest in, European intellectual and cultural history as well as rural and regional history. These include *Countryside: Mirror of Ourselves; When Father and Son Conspire: A Study of A Minnesota Farm Murder; Servants of the Land: God, Family and Farm, The Trinity of Belgian Economic Folkways in Southwestern Minnesota; A New College on the Prairie: Southwest State University's First Twenty-Five Years, 1967–1992; The Great Jerusalem Artichoke Circus: The Buying and Selling of the Rural American Dream;* and, most recently, *At the Headwaters: The 1993 Floods in Southwestern Minnesota*, a study of the origins and effects of the 1993 floods, especially in and around the regional lead city of Marshall.

JOHN W. MEYER

John Meyer is an applied sociologist specializing in public management and finance. He has researched, designed, and managed several significant public development projects in rural Minnesota. With an M.S. in Geography and a Ph.D. in Rural Sociology from South Dakota State University, Dr. Meyer has authored ten critical cultural/demographic reports and three development simulation computer software applications. He has researched and written a series of articles on the impact of development attempts in rural Minnesota.

JOHN RADZILOWSKI

John Radzilowski is a 1989 graduate of SSU, and is ABD in history at Arizona State University. He lives in Minnesota and has written extensively on the history of southwestern Minnesota. He is the author of *Prairie Town: A History of Marshall, Minnesota, 1872–1997* (forthcoming in 1997).

DONATA R. DEBRUYCKERE

Donata DeBruyckere is the coordinator of the Rural/Regional Studies program at Southwest State University in Marshall, Minnesota. In 1991 Mrs. DeBruyckere graduated from Southwest State University with degrees in History and Political Science. In addition to her work at the university, Mrs. DeBruyckere is a homemaker and farmer. Her chapbook, *You Can Never Say We Didn't Try: The National Farmers Organization in Lyon County, Minnesota, 1962–1988,* was published in 1990.

ANTHONY J. AMATO

Anthony J. Amato was raised in southwestern Minnesota. A Ph.D. candidate in history at Indiana University, he is completing his dissertation on peasants in the Carpathian Mountains, where he did two years of on-site research. With a B.A. from the University of Minnesota and an M.A. from Indiana University, Mr. Amato is the author of several articles and reviews in national and international publications.